# CONTENTS

# FOREWORD

The social housing sector makes an unparalleled contribution to the UK's physical and social infrastructure. It does so despite operating in a climate of challenge and change. The recent Barker report, for example, confronts the sector with further questions to resolve.

But central to the future success of social housing will be the sector's ability to secure, motivate and retain an appropriately talented and engaged workforce. Given what we already know about the changing demographic profile of the UK labour market, this will be a difficult task. By 2010, for example, only one in five of the UK workforce will be a white, able-bodied male under 45 years old and in full-time work. Clearly, those employers most likely to thrive in the changing recruitment market of the future will be those who are quickest to adapt to its diversity.

But social housing has some advantages over other sectors. It is widely seen to be made up of ethical employers doing ethical business. There is growing and compelling evidence that these attributes are increasingly important to people when choosing their next employer and when deciding whether to stay or leave. This represents an important aspect of social housing's 'brand' as an employer on which it might trade more assertively.

When facing such challenges, what employers need most is practical support and advice which will make a difference. There is no doubt in my mind that this is what this good practice guide delivers. It represents an intelligent fusion of context-setting, practical source material and real examples which will ensure that it has real impact, and I congratulate the author on this achievement.

*Will Hutton*
*Chief Executive*
*The Work Foundation*

# ABOUT THE AUTHOR

Helen Green is an independent housing consultant. She has worked in housing for more than 15 years, for local authorities and housing associations. Her roles have included front-line delivery of housing services, research and information management and human resources and communications.

Helen's specialisms include research, analysis, performance management and reporting, best value, development of policy and procedural guidance and its auditing for best practice and written communications generally. She is an associate consultant with HouseMark, involved particularly in the validation of housing associations' systems for performance reporting.

Helen commissioned and project managed both stages of a national, Housing Corporation-funded research study into recruitment and retention in the housing association sector. She was the author of the first stage of the research published as *To Have and To Hold* in 2002, with the second stage findings to be published as a Housing Corporation Sector Study in 2004.

**Helen Green**
hmgreen@onetel.com
Telephone 01296 620653 or 0777 618 1680

# ACKNOWLEDGEMENTS

The Chartered Institute of Housing would like to thank the Housing Corporation for providing an Innovation and Good Practice Grant to fund this publication, and to thank David Cheesman, Head of Policy, Research and Statistics at the Housing Corporation for his helpful support and guidance throughout the project.

The project team is indebted to the many organisations and individuals who provided encouragement and feedback on drafts of the Guide, including:

| | |
|---|---|
| Alison James | Gwalia Housing Group |
| Anna Knight | Circle 33 |
| Brendan Fowler | Canmore HA |
| Heather Salway | Eden Brown Recruitment, Training & HR Consultancy |
| Helen Correy | Leeds City Council |
| Judith Leigh | Thames Valley HA |
| Kate Hargreaves | HERA Recruitment Ltd |
| Lisa Burns | Northern Counties HA |
| Lisa Mortleman | Housing Corporation |
| Martin Winn | Chartered Institute of Housing |
| Martyn Pearl | Isle of Wight Council |
| Maureen Taggart | Northern Ireland Housing Executive |
| Melanie Rees | Audit Commission/Chartered Institute of Housing |
| Mick James | Employers' Organisation for Local Government |
| Peter Bush | Housing Corporation |
| Peter Jeffrey | St Mungo Community HA/Anglia Housing Group |
| Susan Laycock | Bradford Community Housing Trust Group |
| Susan Walker | MORI |
| Tony Carruthers | Margaret Blackwood HA |

Thanks are also due to all the organisations and individuals who helped with identifying, providing and verifying the good practice examples.

Steven Lorber at Lewis Silkin Solicitors kindly gave permission for his work to be used in Appendix 1. Marianne Skelcher at Bromford Housing Group gave useful insights in an interview with the author. Tamsin Stirling of Tamsin Stirling Associates Ltd and Peter Dickinson of GHK Consulting Ltd provided helpful comments and suggestions, and several CIH staff contributed to the progress of the Guide, including Alison Roberts, Andrea Johnson, Debbie Larner, Diane Hill, Jill Goult, John Thornhill, Keiran Walsh, Marie Vernon, Marion Conlon, Mark Gibson, Nick Fletcher, Niki Walton, Philippa Russell and Tim Pogson.

# CHAPTER 1

# INTRODUCTION

Effective organisational performance depends upon recruiting, investing in and retaining staff of the right calibre. This is especially true in a staff-intensive sector such as social housing and in an environment of low unemployment, skills shortages and rapid change. Housing organisations need effective strategies in place to ensure they are able to attract and hold on to quality staff.

This is an area where organisations can learn from each other and there is certainly much good practice in the sector. By way of example, in 2003, three housing organisations broke into the prestigious Sunday Times list *100 Best Companies to Work For*. Bromford Housing Group, Pinnacle PSG and London and Quadrant Housing Group beat major household names to be ranked number 5, 63 and 67 respectively. In the 2004 list, London and Quadrant improved their ranking to 29 and Pinnacle reached 43rd place. United Welsh Housing Association reached fifth place in the Financial Times 2004 *50 Best Workplaces* report, with Bromford Housing Group reaching number 13 and Shelter at 38. The Ridings Housing Association and Irwell Valley Housing Association both appeared in the Sunday Times 2004 list of *50 Best Small and Medium-Sized Enterprises*, coming 9th and 17th respectively.

The main theme emerging from the winning projects in the 2003 UK Housing Awards was that 'people count'. Overall winner Tees Valley Housing Group demonstrated through their Corporate Change Programme that a go-ahead housing organisation has to invest in its staff if it wants to make progress. West Lothian Council's Employee Development Strategy and the London and Quadrant Group's Our People Programme reflected a similar theme.

This guide aims to help organisations improve performance in recruitment and reduce their turnover, through highlighting good practice generally, through examining relevant case studies and by pointing to other information and resources which may assist. It aims to challenge some of the dominant HR practices in the sector which, though well-meaning, may be counterproductive.

The guide is not a comprehensive procedure manual for the recruitment and retention of staff. Rather, it starts from the premise that there are difficulties within the sector and highlights the main areas, informed by research and the legislative framework, where organisations may need to concentrate their attention.

A theme running through the guide is the need to ensure equality and the case for promoting diversity, in order to ensure that organisations are recruiting from the widest pool of talent available and are tapping into the potential of all their employees. Examples of solutions appropriate to smaller organisations are also contained throughout the text. It is recognised that small associations, many of which do not employ HR specialists, may face particular difficulties in becoming 'employers of choice'.

A possible criticism of the sector is the lack of collaboration and co-operation between organisations, in terms of attracting and developing staff. Some of the work now under way at a national level is described in Chapter 2. However, there is considerable scope for much greater collaboration and partnership arrangements between organisations in this area. After all, what is good for the sector is likely to be good for individual organisations too. Research shows that existing housing staff want to stay within the sector.

Topics in the guide are addressed largely in sequential order, from attracting and selecting recruits, to integrating and developing them, through to their working conditions and environment. However, the guide emphasises that many of the solutions to the problems of recruitment and high turnover lie at the heart of how organisations are managed. Interventions must be approached from an organisational, strategic perspective and the procedural aspects covered are grounded within this overall context.

Many of the recommendations in the guide involve taking a longer-term perspective. There has been too much short-termism in the past, resulting in problems stored for the future. There are few stand-alone, quick fixes that can be left to HR staff to implement. For this reason, this guide will be of interest to Chief Executives and their senior management teams and board members, as well as HR practitioners and recruiting managers.

# CHAPTER 2

## BACKGROUND

This chapter sets out the context in which housing organisations are looking to improve their recruitment and retention practices and provides:

- A summary of the current labour market
- An overview of housing sector staffing and key research findings
- A summary of the challenges facing housing organisations
- Details of some sector-wide initiatives under way.

## ❏ 2.1 Recruitment and retention in the current labour market

Despite global recession in 2001, employment in Britain has continued to hit record levels. Labour Market Statistics at April 2004 showed the working age employment rate had increased to 74.9%, the highest since records began in 1984, with trend estimates indicating a continued increase. The unemployment rate had fallen to 4.8%, again the lowest since 1984, with trends suggesting that it would continue to fall.

There are several reasons for this strong and stable job market. There have been important changes in labour supply:

- Rising student numbers (meaning later entry into the job market) and the relative success of the New Deal mean youth unemployment has considerably reduced.
- Whilst the level of employment has risen steadily, the total hours worked in the economy has increased more slowly. This is due to both the increase in part-time work, and the influence of the Working Time Directive in reducing the working week across many occupations. The overall result is that organisations have to find more people.

At the same time, labour demand has continued to be quite strong. This is due in part to increased recruitment in the public sector. In the four year period to June 2002, the latest date for which there is comprehensive information, employment in the public sector grew by around 7%. Prior to these gains, employment in the public sector had fallen for over 15 years in a row. Job growth in the economy as a whole continued in the year to 2002, despite the fact that output growth was below trend. The job gains were split fairly evenly between the public and private sectors, but given that the public sector only constitutes about 19% of total jobs, the contribution of the public sector to employment growth was unusually large. Future projections show a slight reversal of this as private sector recruitment will continue to increase, whilst financial constraints imposed by the government on many public sector organisations will lead to slower growth in this sector.

In all sectors, recruiting and retaining skilled staff are major problems for employers. In the CIPD 2003 Recruitment and Retention Survey, 93% of organisations attempting to fill their vacancies experienced recruitment difficulties, (against 77% in 2002). 72% of organisations reported retention difficulties in 2003 (50% in 2002). The job-for-life ethos is becoming more unusual, with employees spending a shorter average time in one job.

High employment has made skill shortages more apparent. There has been a steady growth in the proportion of jobs that are knowledge- or skills-based. There is less low-skilled work, and those jobs that are available increasingly require, especially in the service sector, relatively well-developed social skills. This means it can be harder to fill jobs appropriately. In the CIPD 2003 survey *"lack of specialist skills"* and *"poor quality applicants"* were the main reasons given for difficulties in recruitment across all sectors. The serious skill shortages in certain fields of employment have been well documented, especially within public services such as health, education and social services.

In addition, regional variations in employment levels are set to continue. Institute for Employment Research projections for employment growth to 2010 indicate that the south east, eastern and south west regions of England will continue to experience the fastest increase.

Finally, the balance in the labour force is changing, most particularly with the number of older people available for work. Almost 40% of Britain's labour force will be aged 45 or over by the year 2010, and only 17% under 24 (Equality Direct figures). Women and people from BME backgrounds are set to make up a much greater percentage of the national workforce in the near future. One important consequence of the population changes is the greater number of employees who will have caring responsibilities both for children and older people.

## ❏ 2.2 Employment in the social housing sector

The social housing sector is staff-intensive. The Sector Skills Council for the industry estimates that over 150,000 people are employed in the UK social housing sector.

## Staffing profiles – some facts

The housing association sector has been marked by rapid growth in the past decade, largely as a result of the local authority stock transfer programme and corresponding employee transfer. As at March 2003, 111,785 people were employed by housing associations in England, compared to 49,530 in 1993. The 2003 figure equates to 94,864 full time equivalents (FTEs).
(Source: Housing Corporation RSR 2003 data)

### Gender
Three-quarters (75%) of housing association staff are women. However, the proportion of women in senior positions is considerably lower. In September 2003, in the top 200 associations (by stock), 34% of senior positions were held by women, and there were just 24 Chief Executives (12%).
(Source: Housing Corporation Leadership 2010 report)

### BME
73% of staff are described as White British/Other, a figure which has fallen from 79% since 1993. The absence of BME senior staff is an area of particular concern. BME staff make up just 1.6% of senior staff at mainstream housing associations.

### Age
A MORI survey in 2003 of 1,828 housing association employees in England showed the following breakdown by age:

| Under 25 | 25 – 34 | 35 – 44 | 45 – 54 | 55+ |
| --- | --- | --- | --- | --- |
| 6% | 25% | 30% | 26% | 11% |

Until recently, many housing organisations have done little to attract a younger workforce, tending to rely largely on a 'recycling' of staff within the sector. As a result, many organisations are now faced with an ageing staff group. These figures are comparable with an Audit Commission study of recruitment and retention in the public sector (2002). This research showed fewer young people being attracted to work for the public sector and a potential 'demographic time-bomb' with 27% of the public sector workforce aged 50 or over.

Clearly, whilst recruiting younger workers is of vital importance, the difficult labour market means that the effective retention, development and motivation of older workers is equally important.

---

### Key research findings

Research by Housing Potential UK, then the national training organisation for housing, to inform the Housing Workforce Development Plan published in 2002, showed:

- Acute competition for quality senior managers and concern about where the managers of the future would come from.
- A poor record on training new entrants to housing and a skills gap at lower levels. There was low take-up of vocational qualifications and a lack of training in specialist areas (eg in care and support).
- An ad hoc approach to training within many organisations.
- A high degree of concern about keeping staff skills up-to-date.
- Anecdotal evidence of a reluctance amongst employers to release employees for study.

MORI research into recruitment and retention in the housing association sector in England (2002) found:

- Recruitment was the biggest challenge for HR directors, especially amongst those employing staff in London.
- Retention was placed second amongst the challenges for HR. The average staff turnover was 16% which, though less than the national average, masked wide differences within the sector, with larger associations and those in London experiencing most difficulties.
- Relative ignorance about the social housing sector – over half of members of the public of working age knew not much or nothing about housing associations.
- Mixed views on working in social housing amongst members of the public. Their main impression was that it would mean working with difficult customers. On the positive side, working in social housing was viewed as making a difference to people's lives and providing a worthwhile job.
- Pay was the most important factor for members of the public when choosing a new job, and other important influences were work interest, employment security, and convenience or flexibility.

In a second stage of the research (2003), exploring issues around staff retention, MORI found:

- Staff had been attracted to work in the sector initially by interesting, worthwhile and varied work, the chance to make best use of their skills, convenient/flexible hours and working for an organisation that serves the public.
- Two-thirds of staff would like to stay with their employer for the next two to three years – either in their current job or through promotion. Of those that wanted to change employer, most wanted to stay in the housing or public sector.

→

- Fairly low satisfaction regarding opportunities for personal development. The ratings for line management also reiterated the need for employers to focus on improving career development for their staff.
- A consistent relationship between employee satisfaction across a range of issues and the extent to which staff felt they were kept informed by their employers.
- Three in five people who had recently left a housing association had done so for 'push' rather than 'pull' factors. The main push factors were poor salary, no career prospects or opportunities and a lack of management support.

These findings corroborate a host of other research, across all employment sectors.

Research by Roffey Park Institute (2001) summarised the characteristics of desirable organisations, as places where people:

- Can progress their career
- Feel involved
- Feel equipped to do their job
- Are appropriately rewarded
- Can balance work and home life
- Can learn and develop

Purcell et al in research for the CIPD (2003), looked at HR policies that seemed particularly influential in helping to generate organisational commitment. They identified the key areas as:

- Career development
- Training opportunities
- Job influence and challenge
- Involvement
- Appraisal processes
- Work-life balance

Taylor, in *The Employee Retention Handbook* (2002), identifies some common features in organisations with relatively low turnover:

- High degree of employee involvement
- Investment in training and development
- The opportunity for employees to develop a career internally
- Formal selection procedures
- Team working/devolved decision-making
- Performance-based reward systems

# ❑ 2.3 Challenges facing the housing sector

The social housing sector generally, and housing associations in particular, are facing a period of radical change. This change is taking different forms across the UK and the challenge for the profession has different facets in England, Scotland and Wales. A wide variety of issues are likely, directly or indirectly, to have a major impact on employment within the sector.

- In **England**, by 2005/6, the Government will have doubled, in real terms, its investment in housing compared with 1997/8. The Communities Plan charts a new path for housing associations and local authorities, with new money to boost housing supply in four growth areas in the South and to revive nine failing markets in the North and Midlands. The daunting delivery agenda accompanying such initiatives requires a steady stream of new staff bringing creativity, drive, leadership, strategic thinking and commercial skills.

- The Egan Skills Review, published in April 2004, calls for a cultural change in the skills, behaviours, knowledge and training of more than 100 occupations involved in delivering sustainable communities. The Review, which puts forward a challenging set of proposals for central and local government, planners, architects and surveyors, developers, housing and social services providers and the business and voluntary sector, calls for the development of "world class general skill sets" in areas such as leadership, teamwork, communication and partnership working.

- By 2005, local authorities must have appraised their stock options in order to reach the Decent Homes Standard by 2010. The housing association sector will continue to grow, as further local authority properties move across under the stock transfer programme. The total number of homes transferred since 1988 is expected to reach 1 million by the end of 2005. An alternative vehicle to stock transfers are Arms Length Management Organisations (ALMOs). Existing or proposed ALMOs, under the first three rounds of the ALMO programme, cover just under 550,000 homes, or one in five of all council stock (ODPM figures). At an organisational level, the careful management of employment relationships is essential to ensure the success of such arrangements.

- Increased investment in housing is being accompanied by greater scrutiny, with high-level government reviews in 2003/4 into the role and efficiency of housing associations, the housing market and the construction industry. This, together with recent changes to the inspection regime, illustrates the importance of housing in the Government's agenda and the intention to link resources to reform, improved performance and greater accountability.

- In particular, the response to recommendations from the Barker report, which investigated the problems of Britain's housing supply, will be crucial. The report offers considerable support for the role of housing associations in boosting supply, whilst at the same time challenging associations to improve performance in several areas. Highlighting the many small associations not seeking to expand against their stock, the review advocated the merger of hundreds of smaller associations. Pooling resources will enable the sector to use its assets more effectively to develop more homes.

- In **Scotland** the devolved Parliament made housing one of its early priorities, and a raft of new legislation is now in place bringing changes to homelessness, tenancy management, tenant participation and the local authority strategic role. There are also changes to the regulation of the social housing sector, with Communities Scotland now the regulator for both local authorities and housing associations, and a best value inspection regime under way to ensure the delivery of quality services.

- Emphasis on the physical quality of the housing stock continues, with landlords required to ensure all social rented properties meet the Scottish Housing Quality Standard (SHQS) by 2015, and publish Delivery Plans on progress towards this. From 2004, the Scottish Executive has granted local authorities additional freedom to borrow in order to invest in the housing stock.

- The Scottish housing association sector is increasing both in scale and profile. The Scottish Executive has a target to support local authorities to develop or implement proposals for transferring 70,000 homes to housing associations by 2006. The Glasgow stock transfer in 2003 was the largest ever UK transfer. Figures show that lending to Scottish associations will continue to expand, both through stock transfer deals and funding to allow existing associations to expand.

- Local authorities are taking on a more strategic housing role. They are required to produce Local Housing Strategies that map housing needs and conditions across the authority and produce strategies to address these. Many are also looking to take on the role of housing development enabler by taking on responsibility for development funding from Communities Scotland.

- Community regeneration is an increasingly important issue. Housing associations are being encouraged and funded to engage in wider role activity. Local authority housing can also access a specialist regeneration budget where stock transfer is proposed.

- In **Wales** the importance of housing to the wider economic and social agenda of the devolved Assembly is increasingly being recognised. However, this recognition is not accompanied by the scale of increases in investment seen in England and Scotland. The Welsh housing sector needs to be particularly innovative in the face of increasing housing demand combined with scarce resources.

- The Wales Programme for Improvement, Wales' equivalent of the best value regime, places great emphasis on the capacity of local authorities to identify and tackle areas of risk and drive continuous improvement. The first report from the Audit Commission in Wales on the Wales Programme for Improvement notes that many authorities identified some, if not all, aspects of housing as areas of significant risk. It notes that *"the lack of capable management arrangements has been a significant contributory factor."* It also notes that areas of risk, such as national shortages of housing managers, will require decisions at a national level. Additional competition for staff is created by the fact that many Welsh housing organisations are small, and larger organisations in England can offer more attractive career prospects.

- Local authorities and housing associations in Wales are required to ensure that their homes meet the Welsh Housing Quality Standard by 2012. For local government, the options to achieve the investment required are more restricted than those available in England – stock retention, stock transfer or a mix of the two. Wales' first large scale stock transfer took place in Bridgend in 2003, with forecasts that the Welsh transfer movement will continue, changing the nature of the housing association sector.

- **Across the UK** the way the sector works is changing. Partnership arrangements are increasing. Some organisations are outsourcing part of their operations (eg IT, HR and finance). Such arrangements require different capabilities such as skills in negotiating, commissioning, risk management, contract monitoring and financial management.
- Organisations are working within increasingly tight financial constraints. In particular, the impact of rent control in parts of the country, and on some types of association, will directly affect ability to maintain salary levels.
- Important changes to the way development is procured and funded will mean that for many associations development as a means of growth will no longer be an option. The only way to grow will be by merger, transfer or acquisition. The establishment of group structures to address these arrangements can bring its own complexities (eg staff on different conditions and a lack of clarity amongst staff about their employer).
- The sector is diversifying rapidly, to include a greater range of clients and wider services to people in the neighbourhood (eg youth initiatives, childcare, training and job creation). The skills for new posts, eg in neighbourhood management, need to be considerably broader than those required for the traditional housing role.
- Many organisations within the sector are still battling with the need to change from a provider mentality, process-driven approach to a more results-driven, service-delivery culture. This transition requires flexible staff, with greater customer focus.
- There has been an unprecedented volume of new legislation in the employment field, including family-friendly legislation, increased scope of

anti-discrimination law, employee representation, transfer of undertakings, data protection and the working time directive. Appendix 1 provides a summary of the relevant current and forthcoming legislation. The range of workplace entitlements for employees has expanded rapidly, and one result has been increasing numbers of employment tribunal claims.
- Recruitment shortages, demographic changes and legislative and regulatory requirements have forced diversity up the agenda. This has implications far beyond recruitment, and organisations need to ensure they are able to address the demands for different returns from work that will result from increased diversity (eg in terms of career development and work-life balance).

## ❏ 2.4 Sector-wide initiatives

While the rest of this guide features examples drawn from a range of housing employers developing good practice within their own organisations, the following section highlights some of the initiatives under way to promote change across the sector.

---

**Training and skills development**
Working in housing has changed rapidly in recent years, and in response new Occupational Standards for Housing were approved in 2001 and new NVQ/SVQs accredited. In recognition of growing diversity within the profession, the Chartered Institute of Housing achieved Awarding Body status in 2001 and has developed a suite of Vocationally Related Qualifications. The CIH has also undertaken a review of the Professional Qualification to ensure that students are equipped with relevant knowledge and skills to operate effectively in a dynamic environment.

**Housing's Better Future**
Launched in 2003, Housing's Better Future is the National Housing Federation's flagship initiative to improve both the reality and perceptions of housing association work in England, over the next five to ten years. It is focused on creating a new identity for the sector (to improve profile and raise image), and a commitment to an agenda for change throughout the sector.

The initiative builds on a considerable body of stakeholder research, which revealed an overall picture of individual success by housing associations but one of collective failure. The research found:
- A lack of knowledge about the sector and services amongst the general public
- Blurred distinction between housing association and council housing
- Association with bad neighbours
- Inward-looking associations and a lack of collaboration in the sector

→

---

Housing's Better Future is about associations reaffirming their collective identity. The 'rebranding' of associations recognises the multiple challenges they will face in the future and positions the sector to respond at an individual and collective level. The brand is: *iN Business for Neighbourhoods*.

The NHF is adamant that image can only improve if the reality is there to back it up and Housing's Better Future is about assisting organisations to achieve real cultural change.

Of key importance will be:

- The creation of leadership that is able to understand customer expectations and thrive in an ever-changing environment – leadership will also provide the essential motivation to staff
- Employing experienced, committed staff who see innovation as a key part of their jobs

One of the key commitments made by housing associations pledging to support the iN Business for Neighbourhoods agenda is to be an 'employer of choice'.

### Leadership 2010

Leadership 2010 is the Housing Corporation's initiative to increase diversity across the sector's top jobs and to ensure that the leadership needed for the 21st century is in place. The initiative focuses on the women and BME employees already in senior positions or leading smaller associations, and on recruitment from outside the sector. The programme will:

- Launch and endorse a range of leadership programmes.
- Develop leadership competencies.
- Encourage personal skills development through formal teaching, informal discussion, mentoring, coaching, learning sets and networking.
- Seek to 'break the mould' on recruitment practices, emphasising emotional intelligence and competencies, not just traditional skills and experience. One initiative will be to launch a recruitment pack to assist boards involved in senior recruitment.

### CIH Leadership and Management Development Programme

The CIH and the Community Housing Task Force in association with Warwick Business School has developed a leadership programme for senior managers in housing. The programme aims to focus on the challenges faced by leaders in housing organisations, providing skills and tools to expand ability and confidence. The programme consists of three modules:

- Enhancing strategic leadership capacity
- Negotiating, influencing and partnering
- Market awareness and organisational performance.

→

**Bright Futures, Bright Lives, Bright Careers**
Bright Futures is a joint initiative between CIH, the Housing Corporation and the NHF. It aims to assist individual local authorities and associations with recruitment of staff, by reinforcing housing as a career of choice. The initiative was launched at the Forum 3 recruitment fair in 2003 and was supported by seminars and a CD-Rom available at the event and in university libraries and other careers advice centres.

The CD-Rom sets out the wide range of career opportunities on offer within the sector, emphasises the positives about working in the sector and explores the possible routes in.

**Getting into Housing**
This Guide, produced by Inside Housing, is designed as an introduction to careers in housing for school-leavers, students and mature people, looking for a job where they can make a difference. Case studies from people working in housing are used to illustrate the variety of work available and the prospects for career development.

**Housing Recruitment Forum**
The Housing Corporation has launched a Recruitment Forum, which meets quarterly. The overall aim is to create an opportunity for those involved in recruitment and retention in the housing sector to share best practice. The forum encourages the development of shared initiatives that promote careers in housing and encourage talent management across the sector.

**NHF Recruitment, Retention and Retraining Group**
The National Housing Federation convenes a Corporate Services and HR Directors/ Managers group which meets quarterly. Members share information and co-ordinate staffing initiatives around recruitment, retention and training.

**CIH Regional HR Forums**
The Chartered Institute of Housing is organising a series of regional forums for housing organisations' HR managers in order to raise awareness of changing training and education needs within the sector and how to meet them.

# CHAPTER 3

# ORGANISATIONAL CULTURE AND MANAGEMENT STYLE

This chapter considers the importance of organisational culture and management style on staff recruitment and retention. In particular it examines:

- Approaches to diversity
- Effective leadership
- The importance of the line manager
- Performance management systems
- Development of a team culture
- Communication processes

## ❏ 3.1 Introduction

Organisational culture can be simply defined as 'the way we do things around here'. The culture of the organisation and the style of management can have a significant impact on staff loyalty, performance and ultimately retention. It shapes the attractiveness of the organisation to potential new joiners.

Traditionally, managers in the UK have used an autocratic style of management. There is increasing recognition that such a style fails to get the best from staff and is likely to increase staff turnover. By contrast, an inclusive organisation that encourages staff participation, promotes individual autonomy and shares information, can generate high levels of motivation and commitment and is far more likely to achieve its business objectives. Increasingly, organisations are moving towards the development of people-centred management practices, and these should be reinforced during the recruitment process and throughout an individual's involvement with their employer. The following chapters of this guide describe these practices in more detail, particularly the role that managers play in delivering them.

Changing management culture is a long-term process, requiring the absolute commitment of senior management and an effective means of cascading this through the organisation.

## Bromford Housing Group

Bromford HG was recognised as the fifth best company nationally in the 2003 Sunday Times *100 Best Companies to Work For* award. In addition they have been described as an 'exemplary employer' in their Investor in People award. The Group are in no doubt that it is their people and their unique culture that are the key to their success.

The four dimensions of the Bromford People Vision are:

| Creating a workplace where people really want to stay | Growing our own |
|---|---|
| High morale and satisfaction | Learning is part of work |
| People feel they own the place | Colleagues drive their own |
| Front-line decisions | development |
| Feeling valued | Excellent training |
|  | Managers appointed from within |
| **Becoming an employer of choice** | **Inspirational leadership** |
| Top 100 employer | Fun and inspiring place to work |
| Best total employment deal | Coaches, not checkers |
| Turnover in lower quartile | High trust – no blame culture |
| Lose no-one to competitors | Equality of opportunity |
| Work-life balance |  |

All of the individual elements of the HR work programme (from establishing a colleague sounding board to improving career and succession planning), support the overall vision, with most supporting more than one of the four strategic objectives.

## Tees Valley Housing Group (TVHG)

TVHG's Corporate Change Programme won both the *Outstanding Achievement in Social Housing* and the *Good Practice in Recruiting and Developing Housing Professionals* Awards in the 2003 UK Housing Award Scheme.

The Group manages 4,000 homes across the north east of England but predominantly within the Tees Valley, an area of stark contrast between affluent communities and pockets of severe deprivation and social exclusion.

→

The Group recognised that if it was to make a difference and become the housing and community investment agency it aspired to be, it needed to transform itself internally. The aim was to create a culture of learning and empowerment, resulting in a dramatic change in attitude, with the generation of new ideas and innovative ways of working. The purpose of the Corporate Change Programme was to enable the Group to change its corporate approach sufficiently to be able to say "we don't just have a community investment programme – community investment is the way we do things around here".

In conjunction with a regional consultancy, Banks of the Wear Community Projects, the organisation devised a training programme for all 128 staff, plus the board members and tenant representatives who make up the housing advisory panel. The programme had the dual purpose of helping to change the culture within the Group and developing the new skills needed. A three-tier programme was devised, designed to correspond to TVHG's competency framework for staff and based on individuals' level of contact with communities within their roles.

The Group reports a significant change in the attitude of employees to see community investment as more than just residents' meetings but a whole way of working that is integrated into everything that the organisation does. They believe the key to the successful implementation of the programme was to gain staff understanding, commitment and ownership of the programme. Initial briefing sessions, followed by repeat awareness sessions, were held to discuss the aims, to motivate staff to enable them to see the positive benefits in terms of their own positions, and to alleviate staff concerns. Regular staff newsletters continue to give the programme a high profile.

Significant time and energy was invested in giving support to the operational managers, whose role was crucial for ensuring the right messages reached their teams. This work later contributed to the Group's Communications Strategy.

## ❏ 3.2 Approach to diversity

The business case for achieving an inclusive and diverse workforce is summarised in Chapter 5. A key reason for failure by organisations in this respect is due to conflicting organisational priorities. To ensure that diversity is firmly embedded within the culture of an organisation, it is essential that the senior management team agree about the level of priority to be given to diversity issues and that the ethos and values they wish to promote are disseminated throughout the whole organisation.

To achieve success, diversity needs to be fundamental to the day-to-day work of everyone in the organisation, and not seen as an add-on. Examples of ways in which organisations may achieve this include making an understanding of equality and diversity issues an essential job requirement or identifying key performance measures in relation to equality/diversity for each team or employee.

## Mentoring for Diversity

Mentoring for Diversity is an innovative programme developed by the consultancy Equality in Diversity and supported by the Housing Corporation. During a two year programme senior BME housing professionals act as mentors for senior white executives, to help them promote diversity within their organisations and among their partners. The programme aims to help participants' organisations to:

- Become more attractive to potential BME board members and staff, and more accessible to BME community members and tenants
- Improve the internal culture so that board members, staff, communities and tenants find it rewarding to work with.

## The Chartered Institute of Housing

CIH's equality and diversity strategy *Open to All, Closed to Prejudice* has set objectives which are an integral part of the corporate business plan across all the organisation's activities. The strategy acts as both a statement of CIH's vision and as a tool to help achieve it.

## Housing Corporation

The Corporation is developing a 'diversity test' for use in-house which is applied to every job activity (eg organising a lunch or mailing out a leaflet). The test is a series of questions to ask around diversity issues. When fully implemented, the test will be available to other organisations.

## Northern Counties Housing Association (NCHA)

NCHA have recently introduced a 'Key Players' initiative, where staff can indicate an interest in a particular area of work, including Equality and Diversity. The organisation now has 12 Equality and Diversity Key Players in all locations and across all functions. The aim is for them to be contacted for their views and input into a range of issues.

A large amount of guidance is available to organisations (see Appendix 2) to help with:

- Auditing their current equalities/diversity performance (to act as a baseline from which to measure improvement)
- Adopting, implementing and communicating an equality/diversity policy
- Training to ensure the strategy, policies and procedures are delivered effectively
- Target-setting and monitoring to know whether policies are working.

# ❑ 3.3 Leadership

Leadership has a major role to play in setting the culture and context for attracting, motivating and supporting staff. It is important to recognise the difference between leadership and management:

- *Management* is about keeping the current system functioning – ensuring day-to-day operations work effectively and efficiently
- *Leadership* is strategic and is about creating the momentum to produce and sustain change, in order to realise the vision.

Providing a vision, energising people and enabling them to take action is a considerable challenge, especially in a climate of rapid change. The Institute for Employment Studies highlights four quadrants of 'intelligence' for effective leadership. Improvements in leadership requires attention to all four areas:

|  | Tasks | Relationships |
|---|---|---|
| Strategic development | **Entrepreneurial intelligence** Creating new opportunities and co-ordinating resources to exploit them | **Cultural intelligence** Contributing to shared values, aims and institutions |
| Operational performance | **Professional intelligence** Getting things done to time, to quality, to regulation, to cost | **Emotional intelligence** Getting others to do willingly and well what needs to be done |

IES (2002)

Organisations (and particularly boards and committees when recruiting senior managers) need to recognise that no one person is likely to be strong in all areas. What is important is to develop the capacity of the senior managers both individually and as a team. Taking this wider view of leadership should give the opportunity to widen the recruitment pool both within the sector and outside.

Housing has suffered in the past from an absence of sector-wide leadership initiatives, and other sectors are ahead in terms of recognising and developing the skills needed for the future. Some recent schemes at a sector level were mentioned in Chapter 2. In addition, many housing organisations are recognising the need to strengthen leadership capability and are increasingly embarking upon their own leadership development programmes. Organisations may wish to consider pooling resources for training as the programmes will tend to be similar in content. A critical aspect organisations need to address is the lack of diversity of leaders (see Chapters 2 and 5).

The development of leadership skills is not easily achieved through conventional formal training. There is a growing acceptance of the need to divert managers away from long classroom courses towards learning that is more closely related to their jobs. This has led to an explosion of interest in more personal forms of learning support, including mentoring, coaching, 360-degree feedback, project working and learning sets. These forms of learning, though popular with managers, are labour-intensive to support and can be difficult to evaluate.

The Employers' Organisation for Local Government has produced guidance on the main types of leadership development programme, together with common pitfalls and problems.

· · · · · · · · · · · · · · · · · · · · · · · · · · · · · · · · · · · · · · · · · · · · · · · · · · · · · · · · · · · · · · · · · ·

## Thames Valley Housing (TVH)

TVH delivered a comprehensive Management Improvement, Development and Skills Programme (MIDAS) for Senior Managers and Directors.

The Programme included master classes in the following key strategic areas:
- Culture and organisational performance
- Strategic thinking
- Developing a customer-centred strategy
- Leadership
- Motivation
- Managing change
- Performance management
- Developing high performing teams
- Self-management

The emphasis was on the practical application of the master classes to the work of TVH. The programme included 360-degree appraisal with individual feedback, the development of individual learning plans and one-to-one coaching focusing on improving performance in the workplace.

· · · · · · · · · · · · · · · · · · · · · · · · · · · · · · · · · · · · · · · · · · · · · · · · · · · · · · · · · · · · · · · · · ·

Investors in People (IiP) has produced a Leadership and Management Model, which can serve as a checklist for organisations.

Note: Leadership/management succession is discussed in Chapter 11.

# ❑ 3.4 The importance of the line manager

The relationship between the line manager and the employee is the most important in the organisation, from the point of view of the employee. CIPD research in 2003 found that the more highly employees rated their line managers, the more committed and productive they were.

Research by Taylor for the CIPD (2002) reveals that poor or ineffective line management is often the root cause of decisions to leave an organisation. This is especially true in the public/services sector where the quality of supervision appears to be particularly poor. Taylor concludes that organisations which focus on improving this aspect of their operations can benefit substantially from reduced staff turnover.

## Northern Ireland Housing Executive (NIHE)

NIHE has developed a Management Charter setting out the standards which staff can expect from their manager. It addresses such areas as:
- Information sharing
- Staff involvement
- Listening to, and addressing, staff concerns
- Recognising achievements of staff
- Process for appraisals and a commitment to agreeing Personal Development Plans with all staff.

The Charter is supported by the Management Assessment of Proficiency Programme, to date attended by over 130 managers. Progress against the standards contained in the Charter are monitored using the Staff Attitude Survey and focus groups.

## ■ Principles of effective line management
- Providing regular and objective feedback on performance
- Recognising good employee performance
- Avoiding the perception of favouritism
- Talking to every team member regularly
- Acting on suspicion of problems
- Delegating effectively, so giving people as much autonomy as possible
- Involving people in decision-making

(Adapted from *The Employee Retention Handbook*, CIPD, (2002)

This list concentrates on skills and approaches needed at an individual level. However, the chances of good line management becoming a reality will depend largely on organisational policy and practice. The following sections identify the most important policies organisations need to pursue.

## ■ People management skills

It is often assumed that people who are good at doing their current jobs will be good managers of others doing the same job. This often results in inexperienced managers who are ineffective at motivating and developing their staff.

To recruit effective managers, organisations need to define, and recruit against, the full range of competencies required for each managerial post.

## ■ Effective management training

Being a line manager is a difficult job. Even in the Sunday Times 2003 *Best 100 Companies List*, middle managers achieved lower scores for well-being and higher scores for stress than those above and below them. This was echoed in the 2003 MORI research within the sector.

New, established and potential line managers will need effective training to develop the skills essential for a good manager and to reach the required level of competency. Many organisations in the sector are developing comprehensive management training for all tiers of managers, often with external accreditation.

Organisations too small to run their own management training programmes may consider running schemes in partnership with other small organisations or buying into programmes offered by larger organisations.

••••••••••••••••••••••••••••••••••••••••••••••••••••••••••••••••••••••••••

### Horizon Housing Group and West Kent Housing Association

Horizon HG and West Kent HA have developed a Management Development Programme run jointly with Europa consultants and Ability Professional Training Ltd (APT).The programme aims to provide an accredited route through recognised management qualifications, with an emphasis on management within social housing. The programme is aimed at all tiers of management and managers can progress through various levels, gaining:

- Certificate in Management Studies
- Diploma in Management Studies
- Masters in Management

all accredited by the Chartered Management Institute.

The programme offers modules in leadership, people management, financial management and some housing related modules. To make the programme financially viable, Horizon is inviting a number of other associations to buy in to it.

••••••••••••••••••••••••••••••••••••••••••••••••••••••••••••••••••••••••••

......................................................................................................

## Cube Housing Association Ltd

Cube HA has in place an in-house Supervisory Development Programme.
The six-week programme involves one half-day's training per week on the
following areas:

- Managing today – roles, responsibilities, qualities and skills
- Leadership and teambuilding
- Assertiveness at work
- Time management
- Problem solving and decision-making
- Change and action planning

Following a successful pilot, Cube now runs the programme twice yearly.
The programme is also offered, as a development opportunity, to staff
without line management responsibility but who have expressed an interest
in moving into a management or supervisory role.

......................................................................................................

As discussed under Leadership above, and in Training in Chapter 11, there is an
increasing recognition of the need for learning, by staff at all levels, to be more
closely integrated with day-to-day work. In particular, the technique of on-the-job
coaching is emerging as an important skill for those with management
responsibility and several organisations are seeking to develop this skill in their
managers.

## ■ Performance management system

The importance of an effective performance management system is discussed
throughout this guide – at induction (Chapter 10), as a means of highlighting
training and development needs (Chapter 11) and as the backbone to
implementing contribution pay (Chapter 12). This section considers the importance
of an effective system for encouraging and motivating staff.

An effective performance management system needs to:

- Be driven by the line manager, who will need training in the necessary
  processes and the time and resources to devote to it.
- Provide regular ongoing performance feedback, through a system of 1-1
  review meetings.
- Provide regular formal appraisal, generally annually or six monthly. Ideally
  the main purposes of appraisal – performance review, reward review and
  the developmental aspect, should be separated out as they have conflicting
  aims. If it is impractical to hold separate discussions, it is important to
  ensure that no one aspect is overlooked.

- Ensure clear, mutually agreed performance criteria, drawn from business objectives and competencies. People will not be motivated if they do not know what is expected of them or how their success contributes to the organisation.

- Encourage genuine two-way dialogue between the line manager and the appraisee eg the meeting structure should encourage the employee to prepare in advance and allow them to do most of the talking. There is evidence that if people are given the opportunity to express their concerns, and have them heard, they are less likely to see leaving as their first option.

- Focus on improvement, not criticism or blame.

- Recognise and publicise good individual performance.

- Use objective rating systems and include fairness and consistency checks. These checks can be carried out on a snapshot basis, rather than continuously. Evidence of particular groups of staff doing significantly better or worse than other groups will need investigating.

## Cube Housing Association Ltd

Cube HA has a formal appraisal system based on a competency framework. There are three levels of competency: for estate-based staff (caretakers, wardens and cleaners), for office-based staff (all levels of staff without management responsibility) and for supervisory and management staff.

The scheme encourages staff to self-appraise by completing the appraisal forms prior to interview, and the interview with the line manager is very much an open, two-way process. A 'no surprises' code of conduct ensures that managers highlight any performance issues in advance and that these are not left to the day of the interview.

A recent evaluation of the process has shown that both staff and managers welcome the opportunity to meet formally twice yearly (the annual review meeting and a mid-term review meeting six months later). Staff value the way the process allows better recognition of their contribution to the organisation.

## ■ Assessing line managers

Managers are generally appraised on their success at meeting organisational objectives and rarely on their achievements as managers of people. Managers must understand that their performance in managing staff is a matter of major organisational concern. This can be achieved in the following ways:

- Building line management achievements prominently into their own appraisal interviews.

- Using 360-degree appraisals – whereby managers are formally appraised in terms of their performance by their reportees, peers and line managers.
- Rewarding line managers who are good at developing and retaining their staff.
- Ultimately removing those managers with poor people-management skills and replacing them with managers with the skills set to support and develop their staff. Though unpleasant, and unsettling in the short-term, organisations that are serious about reducing high turnover will need to address this issue. Employees who lack confidence in their manager will leave sooner rather than later.

## ■ Managing diversity

For organisations with an increasingly diverse workforce, it is important that managers are equipped to properly manage this. Organisations need to identify the key competencies in managing diversity for managers and to reflect these in the recruitment process and in training and development programmes. Examples of such competencies may be the capacity of the manager to be non-judgmental about other people, or to demonstrate empathy with others, to tackle problems quickly and to make decisions which are likely to make them unpopular with some team members.

## ❏ 3.5 Team culture

Improving cohesion and loyalty through effective teambuilding can be an important means of helping to recruit and retain staff, as well as improving performance. Team working can:

- Enable a greater degree of autonomy/empowerment
- Provide more opportunity to participate in decision-making
- Be a means of improving diversity (see Chapter 5)
- Develop a strong loyalty amongst team members, so reducing any sense of isolation
- Enable individual team members to develop a broader range of skills

Teambuilding activities can include:

- Setting team performance targets and recognising team performance (see Chapter 12)
- Training (eg in inter-personal skills)
- Project working
- External exercises and informal get-togethers
- Establishing effective internal communications (see below)

........................................................................

## Denbighshire County Council

In 2001 the Council received a 'zero stars, will not improve' rating for its Housing Rents service. The Audit Commission report highlighted high staff turnover and absenteeism, an over-reliance on temporary staff, low motivation amongst staff and poor management.

In 2003 the service was the highest-rated rent service inspection in the UK, and in 2004 it won the housing team category of the Public Servants of the Year Awards. Staff turnover has fallen from 40% to 10%, and the problem of long-term sick leave has been eradicated.

The Council considers the key to this massive turnaround has been team-work and the empowerment of staff. They have encouraged this in a number of ways:

- Although staff have specific areas of responsibility, team rather than individual performance targets are set. This means that if someone is off work, the rest of the team will split the workload between them. All targets are clearly linked to corporate objectives.
- Regular weekly team meetings are used to set targets, review performance, encourage new ideas and update on what is happening in other departments.
- Six-monthly awaydays are held to enable the team to review past performance and to develop the five-year action plan.
- Managers have been keen to ensure that the work of the team has been recognised (eg through tenant publications and the internal staff newsletter).

........................................................................

# ❏ 3.6 Communication

The link between employee communication and morale, motivation and staff retention is well established. The MORI 2003 research into retention in the housing sector showed a consistent relationship between employee satisfaction across a range of issues and the extent to which they are kept informed by their employers.

People need to know what is required of them and how this relates to the overall objectives of the organisation. In addition, they need to be aware of the main issues affecting the organisation. This is increasingly important with the trend towards flatter structures and the devolving of responsibilities to individuals. However, communication must not only be top down, but also flow from the bottom up and laterally. The key to the success of many communications systems is the extent to which they provide for two- or three-way communication.

It is important to distinguish between *communication* and *consultation*. Communication is concerned with the interchange of information and ideas within an organisation. Consultation goes beyond this and involves managers actively seeking and taking into account the views of employees before making a decision.

Having formal communication and consultation channels in place is not sufficient. They will be worthless if, for example, staff perceive that little account is taken of what they say in the staff survey or if they fear the consequences of using the formal grievance policy. Behaviour must be consistent with strategy. Staff must genuinely feel that the mechanisms in place are designed to take account of their views.

The range of internal communication techniques available to organisations includes:
- Open meetings/roadshows
- Team briefing/cascade networks
- Annual staff conferences
- E-mail bulletins
- Intranet
- Staff newsletter
- Notices
- Individual letters
- Meetings with Trades Union/Staff Council
- Managers walking the job
- Staff surveys
- Staff focus groups
- Staff suggestion scheme

The choice of method will depend upon the specific nature of the message, the direction of the communication and the speed at which it needs to be delivered.

---

### Good practice checklist: Improving internal communications

✓ Have a written, internal communications strategy, for informing and consulting with employees. Involve employees (and trade unions) in the process of drawing up the strategy. Ensure it is communicated effectively to staff.

✓ Nominate a senior person with responsibility for the strategy and provide adequate resources and support for the role.

✓ Ensure managers have the information, skills and resources they need to fulfil their roles within the strategy. Ill-informed managers will lose the credibility of their staff. Include training on communication skills in management development.

→

---

✓ Give full and prompt responses to staff enquiries.

✓ Following consultation, give full reasons where employees' views have not been acted on. Equally, where their views have changed something, give due credit and recognition.

✓ Explain why change is occurring. Discuss real concerns and encourage employees to see the benefits.

✓ Share success – whether corporate or individual. Share problems as well as good news – if employees understand problems, they often come up with solutions themselves.

✓ Back up messages with factual evidence.

✓ Ensure the strategy facilitates sharing of information between departments.

✓ Do not ignore the informal channels of communication and the impact these may have on how formal communications are interpreted and understood.

✓ Use more than one medium to successfully communicate and enforce messages. Ensure messages reinforce each other.

✓ Use a variety of media to guard against overloading one communication channel. Be aware of a general communications overload.

✓ Monitor usage and effectiveness of the various communication techniques. Do not assume that because it is 'sent' it is also 'received'.

✓ Where information is disseminated externally, ensure that staff receive information at the same time or sooner than the public and that they have the necessary information to answer enquiries they may receive.

Several organisations produce guidance on developing an employee communication strategy (see Appendix 2).

## Anglia Housing Group

Anglia HG is a geographically diverse organisation, operating over six counties. One of the biggest issues facing the organisation is consistent messaging across the Group. The Group has developed its internal communications in order to:

- Enable the regular, two-way flow of information across the organisation
- Target the communication method to the nature of information that needs to be delivered
- Ensure that business messages are clear, concise, consistent and understood
- Give staff an opportunity to discuss face-to-face with senior managers, issues raised by the information they are given

→

The Group has invested in:
- Developing Core Group Briefs
- Facilitating roadshows – open forums where staff can raise issues with senior managers
- Introducing a company intranet

Anglia reports that the benefits have been significant. The increase in the visibility and openness of senior managers has increased confidence in the messages they are imparting and there has been a reduction in the blame culture that had developed previously.

## United Welsh Housing Association (UWHA)

United Welsh was the first mainstream housing association in the UK to be chosen by the DTI to implement a Partnership at Work project which aims to modernise the way staff work together and actively encourage staff to take charge of their own decision-making. Through the project, the organisation has changed its style of management and consultation processes:

- In an option-based consultation process, UNISON is now involved as a partner at a very early stage in discussing proposed business decisions, rather than being presented with a final proposition on which to negotiate. This approach has been used successfully when organising the opening of a new sub-office and the restructuring of maintenance services.
- Line managers are adopting the same consultation approach to decision-making with their teams, and all staff are encouraged to be more proactive in problem-solving within the organisation.

The DTI Partnership at Work Fund is a grant award scheme designed to improve employer-employee relationships, workplace productivity and job satisfaction.

# CHAPTER 4

# A STRATEGIC APPROACH TO RECRUITMENT AND RETENTION

This chapter considers the need for organisations to adopt longer-term thinking and a strategic approach to the recruitment and retention of staff. This means developing planning processes, linked to organisational needs, and management information systems which provide a sound basis for recruitment and retention action plans. In particular the chapter looks at the importance of:

- An HR strategy, incorporating HR planning
- Measuring and analysing turnover
- Exploring staff aspirations

## ❏ 4.1 Introduction

The Audit Commission, in its 2002 study on recruitment and retention, concluded that the best approaches to effective recruitment, improving retention and making the best use of available staff resources were those that were holistic – seeing action as part of the wider business strategy of the whole organisation, rather than as one-off initiatives.

The research found, however, that many employers were developing recruitment and retention initiatives with vital pieces of information missing. Consequently, many organisations were implementing actions in the hope that they would have an impact but without the evidence and analysis to back up their approach.

This chapter looks in detail at the range of ways of gathering information, and stresses throughout that, whatever the data collection methods adopted, it is vital that the findings are reported and considered at a senior level, so that they may form the basis of an appropriate action plan. With the widespread take-up of schemes such as Investors in People and other standards there is a stronger argument for HR issues to link in as an integral part of organisation-wide strategies.

## ❑ 4.2 Human resource strategy and human resource planning

The aim of an HR strategy is to integrate an organisation's business objectives with its people management approach. An HR strategy should:

- Be based on the overall vision of the organisation
- Identify the people management implications of the corporate objectives
- Set out the key people management objectives and priorities including:
  - employee resourcing
  - learning and development
  - performance management
  - pay and reward management
  - employee relations
  - health and safety
- Outline an implementation plan with clear performance indicators

(Adapted from Employers' Organisation website: Improvement and Capacity Development section)

This approach will ensure that all people management and development activities are relevant and consistent with the organisation's corporate strategic plan.

Human resource planning is an important basic element of such a strategic approach. Traditionally, human resource (or workforce) planning has been about the largely numerical balancing of projected demand and supply of labour, in order to have in place 'the right people, in the right jobs at the right time'. This approach is now viewed as too narrow, and there is growing recognition of the need to incorporate more qualitative issues, such as employee behaviour and organisational culture.

There is no fixed model for producing an HR plan, but it is likely to involve:

- An assessment of where the organisation wants to be, derived from business objectives. This should start with the service outcomes that need to be delivered, rather than the traditional staff establishment that has delivered them.
- An assessment of where the organisation is now, including:
  - a profile of current staff (length of service, age, gender, ethnicity, how far the staff profile is representative of local communities)
  - an 'audit' of skills and competencies of existing staff to demonstrate the resources available within the organisation
  - an analysis of turnover figures, recruitment and promotion trends
  - information from staff (eg on their aspirations and on what they perceive to be the strengths and weaknesses of the organisation).

- A comparison of 'where the organisation is now' with 'where it wants to be'. This will highlight, for example, staff shortages, surpluses and competency gaps thus pinpointing areas for future development.
- An assessment of what is needed to make the transition, and the design of specific action plans that will build the relevant skills and capacity needed for organisational success. For example, specific action plans may include recruitment initiatives, restructuring proposals, training and management development plans, reward plans and communications initiatives.

# ❏ 4.3 Measuring and analysing turnover

Organisations cannot hope to manage their supply of skills without a sound grasp of their employee turnover rates. Without hard data on where turnover is too high for comfort, any intervention strategies will be little better than 'shots in the dark'.

## ■ Significance of turnover

A certain level of turnover is both inevitable and beneficial, bringing in fresh people and ideas and allowing movement within the organisation. However, high turnover levels can cause severe problems – increased recruitment and training costs, reduced productivity, and pressure on the staff who remain. The CIPD (2003) estimates that the average direct cost of labour turnover is £4,300 per leaver, rising to more than £6,800 for a managerial position.

The significance of turnover levels will vary from organisation to organisation. As a general rule organisations should be concerned about turnover levels which are higher than their competitors', or which are rising significantly, in the following circumstances:

- Labour markets are tight, making it hard to recruit people with the skills needed
- Recruitment costs are substantial (eg use of agencies or press advertisements)
- Training has to be provided to new starters at significant cost to the organisation
- A new starter takes several weeks or months to reach full effectiveness in the job, so affecting productivity
- The organisation is growing and does not have spare capacity

(Adapted from *The Employee Retention Handbook*, CIPD 2002).

The target employers need to identify is a level of turnover which is both positive and sustainable for their organisation. Within this, interventions should focus on the higher-risk groups, ie the groups of employees the organisation most needs to keep and where turnover is currently too high. These groups will include:

- Posts where, because of the nature of the work, a vacancy represents a greater loss (eg where the individual customer-employee relationship is crucial)
- Posts which are difficult and/or expensive to fill
- Posts where it takes several months to reach full effectiveness

## ■ Turnover rates

There are several ways of measuring turnover, summarised in the following table:

| Measurement | Comment |
|---|---|
| **Crude wastage rate** <br> Total number of leavers in year to date/total number of employees at date x 100. | Most common measure. Used by CIPD and CBI. Blunt instrument. Fails to take account of unavoidable turnover or length of service. |
| **Voluntary rate or resignation rate** <br> Same calculation as above but excludes those leaving for involuntary reasons (ie temporary contracts coming to an end, involuntary redundancies, dismissals, retirements and ill-health related resignations). | This is the measure local authorities are required to use under best value. |
| **Stability rate** <br> Number of staff with service of a year or more/total number of staff employed a year ago x 100. | Captures distinction between early turnover and turnover of longer-standing employees. <br> Useful for measuring specific attrition problems (eg frequent turnover in a small proportion of posts). |
| **Survival rate** <br> Number of staff recruited in one year/number still employed three years later x 100. | Measures success of the recruitment process and the management of staff. |

It is important that once a decision has been made about which formula will be used and which categories of turnover are to be included, the formula is applied consistently whenever benchmarking comparisons are made. The formula can be applied for the whole organisation and to various groups of employees to determine where particular problems may lie, such as department/location, length of service, age, gender, grade and ethnicity.

### ■ Benchmarking turnover rates

In addition to comparing turnover rates internally, organisations can benchmark their turnover rates externally against:

- Published statistics – national or sector surveys (eg CIPD, CBI, Labour Force Surveys)
- Organisations within a benchmarking club/employers' network
- Organisations selected by direct approach

Benchmarking with similar organisations can allow useful comparisons to be made, provided the calculation methods are robust. Benchmarking processes which allow exploration and discussion beneath the top-line figures are likely to be most effective.

However, it is important to recognise that the key to reducing turnover is to focus on what is happening internally rather than what other organisations are doing.

### ■ Costing turnover

There are several approaches and models for costing turnover. The simplest method is to calculate the obvious direct costs eg recruiting and training a replacement. This level of detail will be sufficient for many organisations and can be presented on a 'not less than' basis.

More sophisticated (and complicated) approaches may seek to:

- Estimate the cost in staff time of administering the recruitment process and covering the vacancy
- Quantify items such as lost productivity
- Take account of cost savings eg unpaid salary

Such an approach may be of value in the case of groups of staff that are highly valued and costly to replace. A detailed analysis of turnover costs may help secure the funds for a targeted retention drive.

### ■ Predicting turnover

Predicting turnover is useful for a number of reasons:

- It provides a robust basis for obtaining funds to implement retention strategies
- It informs the setting of recruitment and training budgets
- It allows realistic targets to be set, eg by department, for reducing turnover
- It helps predicts future skills shortages

There are two main approaches to predicting turnover:

- Making projections based on data collected in the past
- Using management judgement/informed guesswork

Once organisations have an appreciation of overall levels and patterns of turnover, and a prediction of future levels, they can begin to identify information on which to base recruitment and retention strategies. A key part of this must be an understanding of the needs and motivations of staff.

## ❏ 4.4 Exploring the aspirations of staff

To create and sustain a better working environment, it is essential to understand the work experience from the perspective of employees.

However, employers often appear reluctant to 'self-appraise' in this way. Many organisations fail to examine the causes of staff satisfaction/dissatisfaction and causes of turnover, or do so in such an unsophisticated way that the information is not useful in terms of guiding organisational practice. Even where organisations do collect useful information through robust means, research shows that findings are rarely used in any structured way. This general finding was echoed in the MORI 2002 and 2003 research in the housing association sector in England.

There is a range of tools available which, used in combination, will help to build a comprehensive picture of the needs and wants of employees, and thus provide the best foundations on which to build effective recruitment and retention interventions:

- Exit interviews/leavers' surveys
- Stayers' surveys
- Staff surveys
- Information gleaned from 1-1s, appraisals and absence data.

Information gathered through these measures must be properly harnessed and interpreted, and be discussed at senior management team (and board) level. It should be used to inform strategic goals, to agree action and to monitor and review performance. There is sometimes a tendency for survey findings to be dismissed by senior staff not wanting to hear or believe the messages. It is essential that such data is robust, to ensure that it cannot be ignored.

### ■ Exit interviews and leavers' questionnaires

When used effectively, exit interviews/leavers' questionnaires can provide valuable information. They can:

- Identify reasons for and trends in turnover, so aiding employers to target retention strategies
- Identify factors that might persuade people to remain with the organisation (eg changes to terms and conditions)
- Help identify training and development needs of remaining employees
- Be useful in assessing the effectiveness of recruitment and induction processes

- Provide important insights into a job, that may be useful when recruiting a replacement
- Collect information on competitors in the labour market (eg asking the leaver about how terms and conditions compare in the new organisation)
- Provide monitoring information (eg are disproportionate numbers of BME staff resigning?)

There are particular advantages and disadvantages to both approaches:

|  | Advantages | Disadvantages |
|---|---|---|
| **Exit interview** | Shows organisation is keen to hear views of departing employee – may make them feel better about the organisation and less likely to be negative about it. | Information can be inaccurate and unreliable. Most leavers cite pull factors eg 'pay' rather than push factors eg 'dissatisfied with management'. Leavers can be nervous of influencing future references/chance of re-employment. Can mean managers genuinely believe staff turnover to be outside of their control. (See checklist below for how to increase reliability of information). |
|  | Enables reasons for leaving to be properly explored. | May be difficult to gain information that can be collated to identify trends. |
| **Leavers' questionnaire** | Less time-consuming than exit interviews to administer. | There is no guarantee the questionnaire will be returned, especially once left organisation. |
|  | Can design to enable information to be input on a database – easier to analyse and identify trends. | Often no one reason for resigning – more likely to be an accumulation of issues over time. Difficult to express this on a survey form – especially if answering closed questions. |
|  | Individuals may be more honest on paper than face-to-face interview – especially if anonymous and if they have left the organisation. | Inability to probe responses. |

---

### Good practice checklist: Gathering leavers' opinions

**Exit interviews**

✓ The interviewer should be someone with whom there has been no prior reporting relationship and who will not be required to give a future reference (eg HR staff or manager elsewhere in the organisation). An alternative approach is to ask the employee who they would like to carry out the interview.

✓ Timing is important. Exit interviews are best carried out a week or so prior to the last day.

✓ Avoid use of standard questionnaires which tend to prejudge responses.

✓ Allow the employee to explain fully in their own words why they are leaving and what, if anything, the organisation could have done differently which would have led them to remain an employee.

✓ Remember that what matters is what ex-employees actually perceive – not what managers hope that they should have perceived.

**Leavers' questionnaire**

✓ Design is vital. Too many closed questions will generate stock answers. Too many open-ended questions may appear daunting.

✓ Use information from previous exit interviews to shape questions.

✓ Provide clear instructions for completion. Pilot the questionnaire before using it.

✓ Consider timing – post employment questionnaires may be more honest but ex-employees have no incentive to participate and the response rate may be low.

**Both**

✓ Explain the purpose – why seeking the information, how it will be processed and used.

✓ A confidentiality statement may gain a more honest response.

✓ Analyse findings by different groups of employees.

✓ Have mechanisms in place for how the information will be used (eg how will appropriate people receive the information, how can it be used to review existing policy/practice).

---

## ■ Stayers' surveys

Stayers' surveys can provide useful insights by investigating what makes people stay rather than what makes them leave. This approach basically involves interviews or focus group discussions with a sample of employees who are long serving and above average performers, asking them why they have remained employed for so long.

Whilst this will not explain exactly why people leave, it may provide information that can be used to inform recruitment and retention initiatives (eg may reveal the importance of ability to work at home or a crèche facility).

# ■ Staff attitude survey

Staff attitude surveys can provide an excellent overview of employee morale and motivation. By understanding employees' attitudes towards such issues as their jobs, managers and their perceptions of development opportunities, an employer can identify those factors likely to trigger resignations and take remedial action. In addition, useful insights for recruitment purposes might be obtained.

Attitude surveys usually attempt to involve all staff by asking them to complete a written questionnaire. An alternative (or complementary) method is to select a sample of workers and interview them in depth. This allows interviewees more scope to give their views. Such interviews should be conducted independently of the organisation.

## Advantages

- Undertaking a survey can be motivating, by demonstrating to employees that the organisation cares about what they think (although for this to be sustained, the organisation must be prepared to act on the information).
- Surveys can provide an important link between senior managers and the views of staff.
- Regular surveys and the action planning that results from these can provide a framework for improving employee motivation.
- Surveys are a useful way of discovering whether the diverse needs of staff are being met.

## Disadvantages

- Attitude surveys raise expectations, and cynicism can set in if nothing appears to happen in response to the survey.
- To be effective, surveys must be anonymous. This means that the organisation is prevented from identifying and acting on individual problems.

---

**Good practice checklist: Staff attitude surveys**

✓ Success will depend on the design of the survey – this may require specialist help.

✓ Repeat the survey at regular intervals. Every two years is likely to be an appropriate frequency to be able to track improvement/deterioration.

✓ Keep key questions the same to enable comparisons over time.

✓ Ensure sufficient information is included on the form to allow comparisons to be made between different groups of employees.

✓ Consider taking part in a benchmarking syndicate to enable findings to be compared with other similar organisations (see case study below).

→

---

✓ Ensure anonymity. Consider using an external company to increase appearance of objectivity.

✓ Ensure the exercise has the support of senior management and that this is communicated to staff.

✓ Establish at the outset what information is to be collected and how it will be used. Ensure this is communicated to staff so they are clear about the aims and the process involved.

✓ Involve employees in designing the survey form and in planning the survey process, in order to create a sense of ownership.

✓ Publicise findings, and subsequent action plans, promptly and widely. Be upfront about areas of staff dissatisfaction.

✓ Consider exploring key findings further through focus groups.

✓ Consider including a question about intention to leave (eg *do you intend to leave this organisation within the next 12 months?*) Research shows that such questions are good predictors of actual resignations, making it useful to compare responses to job satisfaction questions between those who express an intention to leave and those who do not.

✓ Where the organisation has an intranet, consider issuing and analysing the survey online, to reduce distribution costs and save time in collecting and analysing data.

## ORC International: staff survey syndicate

In 2001, eight London-based housing associations formed a syndicate to survey the opinions of their staff. Assisted by research consultancy ORC International, the group developed a standard questionnaire and survey process. The questionnaire contained 65 questions, in categories such as communications, management, equal opportunities, work-life balance, development and reward and recognition.

Questionnaires were distributed to all staff by each association, but to ensure confidentiality completed questionnaires were sent directly to ORC for analysis.

Each association received their results compared to the syndicate average. Following the success of the pilot the syndicate survey was opened up to other associations and is now used by associations from across the UK.

To enable sharing of good practice, ORC hosts regular meetings where the names of the best scoring associations on key questions are shared within the group and comparisons are made with other sector norms, both public and commercial.

## Northern Counties Housing Association (NCHA)

Following their tri-annual organisational health questionnaire, NCHA develops a joint action plan in partnership with its staff council. The plan allocates work to the management team and staff council, with clear timescales and resources. Progress is communicated to staff via the intranet and staff council meetings.

## ■ Information gathered in 1-1s and appraisal interviews

A further useful source of information is that gleaned in 1-1s and appraisal interviews. A frequent comment by leavers in the sector (MORI, 2002) was that they had raised their concerns previously with their line manager but these had not been acted upon.

Regular meetings within the performance management system which allow two-way dialogue are important at an individual level, as discussed in Chapter 3. They are also a source of staff feedback which is important at an organisational level, and organisations need to establish mechanisms for recognising common concerns.

## ■ Absence data

Use of absence monitoring data can also be useful, in that staff absence can be a sign of individual dissatisfaction prior to leaving a job.

## Servite Houses

The association has been proactive in their measures to retain good and valued staff within Care Services. In particular they have sought to concentrate on what existing staff are telling them. Initiatives include:

- Requiring managers to be alert to potential leavers and taking preventative action
- Not accepting resignations as a *fait accompli* but quickly following up reasons given, to see if they can persuade the person to stay
- Taking a more rigorous approach to collecting and acting on feedback from leaver interviews
- Identifying measures they can take to prevent good staff leaving (eg organising shifts around family/carer responsibilities).

Servite has appointed an HR officer whose main focus is retention and recruitment (in that order). They believe the post has the potential to pay for itself several times over in Care Services alone by maximising the number of permanent staff in post, reducing recruitment and induction costs and minimising reliance on agency staff.

# CHAPTER 5

# RAISING THE PROFILE

This chapter explores:

- How organisations can, via promotional work and partnership ventures, raise the profile of the sector and help create demand for careers in housing
- The need to improve the image of working in the sector, through more sophisticated marketing and through selling the strengths of working in housing
- How to target under-represented groups and increase diversity within the sector

## ❏ 5.1 Introduction

Changes across the housing sector and the increasing diversification into new areas means housing organisations can no longer rely on recruiting from the existing pool of experienced housing professionals. New types of people, bringing new talents and experiences, are needed. To enhance the ability to recruit from different sectors and new groups, organisations must find innovative and creative ways of promoting the sector and jobs within it.

Chapter 2 outlined some national initiatives under way to promote housing as a career of choice. There is much organisations can do at a local level, both individually and in partnership. Such approaches involve taking a longer-term and strategic perspective on recruitment, and organisations need to balance improvements in the longer term against the short-term costs and possible pressures on staff time.

## ❏ 5.2 Creating future demand

### ■ Recruitment fairs

Many people are unaware of the range of jobs on offer within social housing. Recruitment fairs are an opportunity to introduce the sector, thus increasing interest and potential applicants. Such events may be particularly useful for smaller organisations lacking the resources for more expensive recruitment initiatives. One option for smaller organisations is to exhibit in partnership with another organisation in order to share costs.

Attending recruitment fairs will provide the opportunity to:

- Raise the organisation's profile as a main player
- Present the human face of the organisation and talk informally about what working in housing is really like
- Gain impressions from potential applicants about their preconceptions of housing
- Depending on timing, fill real vacancies

## Forum 3

Forum 3 is the UK's largest recruitment and volunteering event for the not-for-profit sector, held annually in London. In 2003 over 14,000 people attended the fair over two days and over 100 organisations exhibited. The Housing Corporation, CIH and NHF have worked together to ensure social housing has a high profile, providing sessions on, for example, getting into housing, corporate job opportunities, and care and support.

## East Thames Housing Group

East Thames Housing Group was one of 32 housing associations exhibiting at Forum 3 in 2003, and reports considerable success. In 2002, they had used the fair largely as a promotional venture. For 2003, they geared up in advance to use the fair to fill real vacancies. Their stand displayed the range of jobs available.

Visitors were invited to fill out a two-page mini-application, highlighting which job areas they were interested in. For some posts, applicants were invited to mini open-days which included job interviews. Others were shortlisted for interview on the strength of the information provided on the pro-forma.

The Group has filled 12 posts as a direct result of the event. In addition, the Group reports growing awareness of the organisation following the fair, demonstrated by considerably increased hits to their website.

••••••••••••••••••••••••••••••••••••••••••••••••••••••••••••••••••••••••••

## Canmore Housing Association

Canmore HA piloted a Trade Recruitment Fair, within their own workshop environment, for in-house maintenance operatives. Following general advertisement, 150 people attended the fair from different trades. On arrival, potential applicants completed a brief pro-forma and met with a supervisor from their respective trade for a short interview. The second stage involved a more thorough interview with the manager and a representative from HR. All vacancies were filled. Canmore cite a number of particular benefits:

- Prospective applicants given the opportunity to see the working environment
- Excellent PR for future applicants
- Greater involvement of supervisors in the recruitment process

••••••••••••••••••••••••••••••••••••••••••••••••••••••••••••••••••••••••••
••••••••••••••••••••••••••••••••••••••••••••••••••••••••••••••••••••••••••

## Pennine Housing 2000

Pennine has been the lead sponsor of the borough's annual Jobs Fair for the past three years, with attendances of up to 3,000 people. The sponsorship demonstrates Pennine's commitment to local community regeneration and investing in the local economy, and is a very cost-effective way of raising the profile of the association.

••••••••••••••••••••••••••••••••••••••••••••••••••••••••••••••••••••••••••

## ■ Liaison with schools and colleges

Maintaining contact with schools and colleges is an excellent way of:

- Raising the profile of housing as a career, promoting the work of the organisation and highlighting roles available
- Increasing knowledge about the needs of client groups
- Challenging traditional stereotypes about certain jobs (eg typical male/female roles)
- Raising awareness of individual organisations' needs for school/college leavers with particular skills and abilities
- Developing employee management, communication and social skills amongst existing staff

Organisations might consider:

### *Primary school children*

- Liaising with schools to link local projects (eg new development schemes) with the National Curriculum

### Older pupils/school leavers/students

- Offering students work experience or job shadowing
- Holding open days/participating in 'insight into industry' or 'workwise' days
- Making careers presentations at schools/colleges and attending careers fairs
- Giving advice on job applications and offering mock interviews
- Participating in mentoring programmes in schools

........................................................................

## SOHA Housing

SOHA is one of the largest housing associations in Oxfordshire. Within a buoyant local employment market which offers relatively high wages, SOHA has had to consider some innovative methods to become an 'employer of choice'. One approach has been to work closely with schools and colleges. Initiatives include:

- Producing a brochure, aimed specifically at school leavers, explaining what housing associations are, giving information on SOHA and focusing on particular roles.
- Offering work experience places for local students.
- Creating four trainee posts in finance, surveying and administration, aimed at school leavers. The posts were advertised in local media and through posters in schools, colleges, youth clubs and leisure centres. Part of the enhanced benefits package to attract the new recruits included SOHA paying for them to pass their driving tests. Over 90 applications were received and the four posts were filled. Each recruit has a personal training and development plan aimed at providing them with professional qualifications.

........................................................................
........................................................................

## Canmore Housing Association

Via Careers Scotland, Canmore HA offers work placements to local high schools each year. The students are allocated a mentor and are offered the opportunity to experience different departments. The initiative has been successful in its aim of attracting younger people into housing and a further benefit has been the mentoring opportunity the scheme provides for existing staff.

........................................................................

···································································

## Milton Keynes Council

The Council is one of five large local employers who set up the Equal Choices Schools Initiative, with the aim of reflecting more fully the local ethnic community profile in its workforce. The programme works with Year 9 students from BME communities to increase their awareness of the job and career opportunities available to them.

The programme consists of an 'introduction to work day' within one of the participating organisations, followed by a 'work-shadowing day' with a mentor from that organisation.

The scheme has provided personal development opportunities for existing employees, both in mentoring young people and in valuing diversity.

···································································

Several organisations which can assist in building links between schools and businesses are listed in Appendix 2.

## ■ Developing the local workforce

As well as contributing to the positive image of organisations overall, there are several reasons why housing organisations should consider providing training and employment opportunities to their residents and local communities:

- Housing organisations are often key stakeholders in local communities – they have a role in promoting social, economic and environmental well-being.
- Initiatives which aim to help low-skilled groups find work, may also have the effect of helping alleviate the organisation's own recruitment difficulties. Schemes such as the New Deal provide NVQ training, at no cost to the organisation. Local labour training schemes are particularly useful in creating a pool of local construction skills.
- Research has shown that social housing tenants are often interested in working in the housing field. In addition, they can offer valuable experience as service-users.
- Such initiatives can improve the diversity of the workforce, making it more representative of the local community.
- Involving local people in their local area can increase pride in community and decrease the likelihood of vandalism and crime.

Reading Borough Council has produced good practice guidance for housing organisations wishing to improve the economic situation of their tenants through training, volunteering and employment opportunities. Warden Housing Association has produced a good practice guide on local labour in construction.

## Southern Housing Foundation

Southern Housing Foundation, part of Southern Housing Group, has teamed up with recruitment company At Work to fund the 'Moving On Up Project' mobile job bus. The converted bus, staffed by a team of five which includes local people who know the area, and equipped with computers, takes employment initiatives direct to unemployed people concentrated in deprived areas of London. It aims to assist unemployed residents in gaining access to real jobs, offering good salaries and with potential for training and development.

The project aims to find jobs for 100 people in the first year. A key element of the success of the mobile centre lies in it not being seen as an 'institution'. It is able to reach individuals unable to visit job centres or who may be uncomfortable dealing with various authorities.

## Novas-Ouvertures Group

Following a successful pilot, the Novas-Ouvertures Group expanded its scheme to employ homeless hostel residents and service users as fully-paid support staff.

The scheme is open to up to 40 participants, who are employed as paid hostel support workers, receiving training and support and working towards NVQs. At the end of the programme, they have the opportunity to apply for permanent jobs.

In addition to developing excellent staff, the scheme is an important part of the Group's drive to move away from the traditional 'welfare' model of service provision towards a 'partner enabler' model, so enabling individuals and communities to achieve their potential.

The scheme has grown to include administration, service user involvement, recruitment and Supporting People posts.

## The Guinness Trust

By developing a range of training and employment initiatives, the Guinness Trust is committed to improving the employment prospects of its residents. In the north east of England, the Trust has taken on tenants as grounds maintenance trainees. The scheme has proved so successful they are now providing services for other associations and a local business park. A key aim is to encourage community involvement in its widest sense, and to concentrate such initiatives in areas where benefit dependency is highest.

## West Lothian Council

The Council encourages tenants, as well as staff, to attend its foundation training course covering basic housing issues (see also Chapter 11). This course has been accredited by CIH and is delivered in partnership with West Lothian College. While the Council found that initially tenants were wary about 'going back to the classroom', the programme has been successful and provides tenants with an opportunity to apply, with a relevant qualification, for jobs in housing. Existing communication links have been strengthened and a better insight has developed into the housing role and the needs of tenants.

## ■ Employing volunteers

One route into employment for potential staff is gaining volunteer experience. As well as addressing key issues such as social inclusion and active citizenship, volunteering can bring clear advantages to employers:

- Volunteers can offer fresh perspectives, an independence of viewpoint and a diversity of experience
- They can provide a pool of potential employees who have acquired some relevant experience and have demonstrated commitment
- The management of volunteers can provide development opportunities for existing staff.

Local authorities, particularly social services departments, have a long history of employing volunteers. Housing organisations may need to consider how they can facilitate and support volunteers. Useful organisations who can assist are listed in Appendix 2.

## ❏ 5.3 Selling housing's strengths

### ■ Employer branding

The housing sector is often criticised for unsophisticated marketing, advertising and communications. This is important at a sector level, and the NHF's rebranding initiative as part of Housing's Better Future has been discussed in Chapter 2.

Branding is also crucial at organisational level. In a sector where organisations tend to be quite similar, there is a need for individual organisations to differentiate themselves from their competitors and to promote themselves as an employer of choice.

Employer branding is about applying the techniques of consumer branding to an organisation. The main aim is to develop a strong and recognisable 'brand' in order to attract new recruits, but it can also improve retention of existing staff if it leads to their greater appreciation of the organisation. It aims to develop a connection in the minds of potential employees between the idea of working for the organisation and certain positive values. Job adverts are a powerful vehicle here, as they convey a public image of the organisation which makes an impression, good or otherwise, on a far wider audience than the potential candidates targetted. Ultimately the goal is for people to feel more positively about their organisation, than they do about other employers.

It is essential to realise that an employer brand cannot be built simply through the advertising images and messages. Making unfounded claims is likely to have a negative effect by generating cynicism and mistrust. There must be a 'perceived reality' behind the claims that are being made, as illustrated below.

---

### Good practice checklist: Employer branding

✓ Find out what existing and potential employees like about the organisation (eg through running employee focus groups or surveying job applicants).

✓ Determine what sets the organisation apart from its competitors (eg its record of investing in community development initiatives, its culture and values, or even the fact it is situated in a beautiful part of the country).

✓ Find the appropriate language and images (ie ones that match your organisation) for broadcasting these distinguishing features.

✓ Communicate these messages at every opportunity (eg through press releases and articles, corporate publications, tenant newsletters, exhibition stands). Remember the role staff can play as the public face of the organisation.

---

## Family Housing Group

Family HG hired advertising agency GWH to assist with their employer branding process. Whilst recruitment advertising was Family's main focus, the brief developed to a wider branding exercise, incorporating their corporate literature, exhibition stand, direct mail and communication to key stakeholders. The Group recognised, through a survey of stakeholders, that despite a good track record, their profile was not as high as it should be and identified the need for a strong, consistent, single voice.

There were two objectives: to attract higher calibre individuals and to bring the image of the Group up to date. Family reports success on both fronts. They estimate the new style of advertisement has increased costs by 20%, which has been more than outweighed by the difference in impact. For Housing Officer advertisements (a post they have had difficulty filling in recent years), they have received 50% more applications through the new, striking visual approach.

Guidance on commissioning external agencies is provided in Chapter 7.

········································································

## Charter Housing

Charter Housing found a different method to raise awareness of their organisation by approaching their annual report in a new way. Their aim was to reach a wider, more general audience, rather than the normal recipients of the report who already knew about the organisation. In place of a traditional report, the association arranged for an eight-page insert in the local paper. The insert included general information about Charter Housing and gave details of job opportunities. The benefits have been two-fold – the association's profile has been raised and the brochure attracted new job applicants and board members.

········································································

## ■ Promotion of roles

The 2002 MORI research into recruitment in the sector gave several insights (both positive and negative) into the perceptions of the general public about working in social housing, including:

- It would be a worthwhile job and one that could make a difference to people's lives
- It would mean working with difficult members of the public
- For people currently employed in the private sector, it would be old-fashioned and bureaucratic.

There was a lack of understanding of the nature of many jobs, with people expressing a greater interest in roles such as customer service, providing support to vulnerable people, improving public services or community development, than in social housing in general.

The 2003 MORI research revealed that existing association staff cited interesting work, making the best use of skills, the ability to accomplish something worthwhile at work, convenient hours and varied tasks as the main reasons they had been attracted to work in the sector.

There is much here that organisations can build upon:

- The large increases in investment in housing, regeneration and neighbourhood renewal are a real opportunity to sell the dynamism of the sector and the exciting roles on offer, eg by promoting key roles in the rejuvenation of cities.
- The huge investment in IT in the public sector and the move to e-government, means some cutting edge projects are under way.
- There is a need to sell a setting where commercial skills can be applied – a commercial business with a social purpose will be an attractive proposition to many people.

- Organisations should move away from describing roles in terms of the social housing sector. They should focus on specific aspects of the work (eg its people-centred approach, the role in developing sustainable communities or in providing support to vulnerable people).
- Organisations should stress the enormous variety of roles and career paths available within the sector.
- There is a need to challenge the negative stereotype that housing is about managing failure, by emphasising the positives (eg tackling important social issues and improving people's lives).
- Personal fulfilment and job satisfaction are further areas to build upon.
- Smaller organisations have additional selling points related to their size. They can promote, for example, the possibility of gaining real responsibility early on, the opportunity to experience how different aspects of the organisation work or the ability to have an influence on the organisation's success.

## ■ Promotion of employment package/terms and conditions

Although the housing sector may not be able to compete with the private sector on pay, it has a good track record as an employer, and organisations are often able to offer an attractive employment package (see Chapters 11, 12 and 13). Examples of features that housing organisations can promote include:

- Job security – this is something valued by a large percentage of the public, but rarely mentioned in recruitment literature.
- Flexible working arrangements and family-friendly policies. Many housing organisations are ahead of the private sector, especially in terms of opening up such benefits to all employees and not just those caring for young children.
- Pension provision – this is an excellent feature which local authorities and those housing associations offering final salary schemes can highlight.
- Generous holiday entitlement
- Training and development packages.

### Telford and Wrekin Borough Council

The Council's flexible working arrangements have helped achieve two awards (see Chapter 13). Their recruitment material clearly highlights their family-friendly policies. In addition, when candidates have to travel to the area for interview, they are invited to bring their families and are provided with overnight accommodation. Advice is provided on local housing, schools and other amenities.

## London and Quadrant Housing Trust

L&Q were winners of the *Best initiative to raise social housing's profile* in the 2003 UK Housing Awards for their initiatives to attract, retain and develop staff.

A *Benefits for Our People* leaflet summarises the impressive list of benefits the organisation provides, under the following headings:
- Core benefits (available to all staff)
- Rewarding our people (detailing the ways in which the Trust recognises and rewards staff)
- Family friendly schemes
- Excellent training and development
- Voluntary benefits (detailing a range of competitively priced voluntary products and services that the Trust has negotiated with suppliers).

The leaflet is available for prospective employees to download from the Trust website.

## ■ Being realistic

Providing a realistic description of the job and the organisation is fundamental to effective recruitment, selection and retention. Organisations need a recruitment message that presents the job in a positive but honest manner.

It is necessary to be upfront about any major features of the job or the organisation that might be considered negative by many people. Failure to do so will mean rejection of job offers or early turnover, when the reality is discovered. Where turnover in a post is a problem, it is important to find out from staff why they are leaving. It is also useful to talk to those staff who have stayed in the job about what they consider to be the positive and negative features. This information can then be used to inform the recruitment campaign.

## Audit Commission

Recruitment packs for Housing Inspectors contain *An Inside View* written by existing postholders, which are honest accounts of both the positive and negative sides of the work. Positive quotes are balanced by mention of the long working hours, time spent away from home in hotels and some of the frustrations of the role.

# ❑ 5.4 Targeting under-represented groups and promoting diversity

Many organisations have developed equal opportunities policies to promote fairness and ensure protection for under-represented groups. In recent years, there has been a shift away from the traditional equal opportunities approach to one of promoting diversity. Diversity takes the principles of equality and applies them to the community as a whole, rather than 'just' the protected groups.

The strong business case for improving diversity in organisations within the sector is well documented:

- An inclusive and diverse workforce will present a positive image of a good and fair employer to potential recruits, and helps organisations become an employer of choice.
- Recruiting a diverse workforce will ensure a wider choice of applicants by making use of all available talent and will bring different outlooks, knowledge, experience and expertise.
- The sector is facing a period of significant change, requiring new ways of working. Organisations embracing diversity will be better able to build a more flexible and multi-skilled workforce, capable of adapting to change.
- A workforce that reflects the sector's customer base, at all tiers, will be better equipped to deal with the range of needs and aspirations of service users, leading to improved service delivery and bringing a competitive advantage. Projections show an increase in the growth of households led by women. Similarly, the BME population is growing. There is great disparity between the numbers of women and BME tenants and front-line staff, and the mainly white, male leadership in housing associations and local authorities.
- An inclusive approach will result in a more motivated workforce which feels valued and willing to contribute to the success of the organisation.

## ■ Legislative framework

Aside from the moral and business cases for ensuring equality and promoting diversity, employers who fail to address these issues risk breaking the law.

Anti-discrimination law is steadily increasing in scope. It is illegal for employers to discriminate against applicants on the basis of sex, disability, race, sexual orientation, religion or belief. Disability discrimination laws are being strengthened and legislation is being extended to outlaw unfair discrimination at work on the grounds of age. A summary of current and forthcoming legislation is included in Appendix 1.

Consequences of failing to comply with anti-discrimination legislation are severe. For example, compensation for religious discrimination and sexual orientation claims is unlimited, and organisations should also consider the damage to their reputation.

## ■ Practical methods of improving diversity in recruitment

### *Take a step back*

Confirm that the organisation can manage diversity, before going out and trying to attract a diverse workforce. It is important for organisations to recognise that they cannot manage everyone in the same way. Consider the implications for areas such as induction, training and development, communications and flexible working arrangements.

### *Role requirements* (See also Chapter 6)

- Appoint people who have potential to grow, but might not currently have all the attributes required.

- Take account of a broad range of qualities, such as transferable personal skills and experience gained outside the workplace.

- Ensure that the job profile only contains requirements clearly related to the duties of the post (eg organisations should not request a higher level of education qualification than is needed). Overseas qualifications which are comparable to UK qualifications should be acceptable as equivalents.

- Ensure that applicants understand what the post actually entails so allowing them to consider whether, for example, there is a possibility the job may conflict with their religious convictions. This will enable them to make an informed decision about whether to apply.

- Consider a 'team recruitment' approach (see example below). A growing body of evidence suggests that diverse teams are more creative than teams whose individuals share similar outlooks and skills.

••••••••••••••••••••••••••••••••••••••••••••••••••••••••••••••••••••••••••••••••

### London Borough of Camden

As part of its Valuing Diversity in Employment project, Camden introduced an innovative approach based on recruiting people to teams rather than concentrating on an individual person specification.

The aim is for individuals to bring much-needed skills that complement those possessed by existing team members. By adopting a creative and less bureaucratic approach Camden expects to be better equipped to meet future development and change, and to successfully meet the needs of the community it serves.

••••••••••••••••••••••••••••••••••••••••••••••••••••••••••••••••••••••••••••••••

## Advertising

- Consider all vacancies for targeted advertising beyond mainstream media to reach under-represented groups (eg use of specialist disability magazines, BME press and websites).
- Ensure the advert appeals to all sections of the community using positive images and wording and avoiding stereotyping. Avoid phrases which imply age restrictions such as 'mature person' or 'young graduate'.
- Actively state that certain groups are under-represented in the organisation and that applications are encouraged from those groups (emphasising selection will be on merit).
- Where there is a Genuine Occupational Requirement (GOR), eg under the Sex Discrimination Act for a specific sex to be recruited, this should be identified at the beginning of the recruitment process. Advertisements should clearly show that the employer considers a GOR applies and should quote the relevant section of the Act. (Note: where a GOR has been used in the past it should be re-examined when the post falls vacant to see if it still applies).
- Commit the organisation to the requirements of schemes such as Positive About Disabled, Age Positive, Commitment to COFEM, and use their accreditation symbols.

## ASRA-Midlands Housing

ASRA-Midlands, a medium-sized BME association, was aware there was a danger of 'cloning' within their workforce and of being stereotyped externally. In response they have reviewed and updated their recruitment and selection policy with a view to encouraging a more diverse workforce and a greater representation of women at more senior levels. The policy addresses the importance of appealing to all sections of the community using positive images and wording, and of targeting advertisements (eg in specific publications/areas) where certain groups are under-represented. The association reports an increase in non-BME applicants and a greater aspiration amongst female employees towards senior positions.

## Recruitment practice

- Operate policies which go beyond basic legislative requirements.
- Be proactive in issuing the organisation's equality or diversity policy to applicants. This will make applicants feel confident that it is an open marketplace and may discourage those whose attitudes do not embrace equality of opportunity.
- Review the impact of current recruitment practices on equality/diversity (eg the use of recruitment consultants).

- Where reasonable, adapt methods of recruitment so that anyone who is suitably qualified can apply and attend for selection (eg reasonable adjustments for disabled people, flexibility around interview times allowing avoidance of significant religious times). It is good practice to invite applicants to make any special needs known.
- Check that any tests used are 'culture-free' (see Chapter 8).
- Train interviewers in equality/diversity issues. Ensure the recruitment panel reflects diversity criteria (see Chapter 8).
- Provide recruitment documents in alternative formats (eg large print or audio).
- Consider staff referral schemes which encourage improved diversity (see Chapter 7).

### Conditions
- Consider single-status working conditions (the same for white and blue collar workers). This can help to attract women to less traditional roles.

### Positive action
Within the framework of an equal opportunities policy, consider:
- Targeting local community organisations (eg to attract people from a particular BME background under-represented in the workforce)
- Using employment agencies in areas where under-represented BME groups are concentrated
- Single sex training schemes (eg to help women returners to work or to help women (or men) gain confidence or attain standards to apply for promotion)
- PATH and other local training schemes aimed at increasing representation from under-represented groups (see Chapter 9)
- Targeting liaison programmes with schools/colleges in areas where under-represented BME groups are concentrated

## Pathways to Housing

The Pathways project developed and ran a modular pre-employment course over a two-month period in Cardiff for members of BME communities, with the aim of encouraging more diversity in the housing profession. The project was developed jointly by Taff HA, Cardiff Community HA and Cadwyn HA in partnership with the Chartered Institute of Housing Cymru.

The course provided a basic understanding of housing management, regeneration, development, maintenance, finance and supported housing.

→

The 11 tutors were volunteers, mostly senior staff with many years' experience in the field, and each participant was offered a personal mentor for up to one year. In addition, front-line staff took part in a jobs fair and talked to course participants about the reality of day-to-day work in housing.

Following the course, more than half of the participants have secured jobs in housing or undertaken work experience placements, and several organisations now include Pathways participants on their circulation lists for job opportunities. The profile of housing organisations and career opportunities has successfully been raised among BME communities in Cardiff and beyond.

## Willow Park Housing Trust

Willow Park HT has sought to redress the gender balance in its previously all-male maintenance service and improve employment prospects in a deprived area. The Trust has set up an apprenticeship scheme for women to train in plumbing and gas appliances.

The scheme was publicised through schools, job centres, libraries and its own offices. The Trust aimed to take on a minimum of three female apprentices to ensure they would not be isolated. Conscious of a likely high drop-out rate, there was a six-month lead-in time so the women were clear what would be involved. Question and answer sessions were held and potential apprentices were invited to taster sessions and days shadowing Technicians.

Six women were taken on to the scheme which lasts four years. Training takes place one day a week in the local construction centre. The remaining time is spent on site with the Willow Park's trades team to put learning into practice, under supervision. Apprentices reach NVQ level 2 in plumbing after two years and NVQ level 3 in domestic gas appliances during years three and four. They receive a salary and help with training costs, buying tools and childcare.

## Nashayman Housing Association

Through their *GO-FOR-IT – A Career in Construction* project, Nashayman HA is working with groups that are under-represented within the construction workforce. Working closely with local training suppliers and construction companies, the project provides initial training and mentoring support to enable women and young people, including those from BME communities, to secure a craft or technician apprenticeship.

### *Monitoring*

- Set recruitment targets to achieve a workforce reflective of the local community.

- Monitor recruitment and staffing figures at all tiers to gain data on gender, ethnic origin, disability and age. For local authorities it is a statutory duty to monitor ethnic origin (see Appendix 1). Note: under the Employment Equality Regulations 2003, there is no requirement to keep monitoring information on religion or sexual orientation.

- Identify any areas that may need particular attention, investigate underlying causes and seek to remove any disadvantage.

- Communicate areas of under-representation to all staff involved in recruitment.

## Tenants First Housing Co-operative (TFHC)

TFHC is the largest fully mutual housing co-operative in Britain. For each recruitment exercise, the success of each recruitment source/advertisement is analysed in terms of initial responses, completed applications, number of candidates shortlisted and appointments made.

Monitoring is carried out against all completed applications, shortlisted candidates and successful appointments in terms of gender, disability, age and ethnic origin.

Results of the monitoring are compared against the Co-operative's performance targets for the recruitment of people with disabilities (currently 6%) and people from a BME background (taken from census figures for the regions concerned). This monitoring information is reported to the Management Team, Staffing Sub-Committee and Management Committee annually.

Details of organisations providing further guidance and assistance on issues around diversity in recruitment are listed in Appendix 2, including sources of advice on particular under-represented groups.

# CHAPTER 6

# DEFINING THE ROLE AND CANDIDATE SKILLS

This chapter emphasises the need for each recruitment decision to be linked to the achievement of the organisation's aims and objectives (ie the need to match people to skills ... to roles ... to business needs). It considers:

- Undertaking a thorough review of each vacancy prior to recruitment
- The importance of clearly defining the role and type of candidate required
- The increasing tendency for organisations to adopt a competency-based approach to recruitment

## ❑ 6.1 Reviewing the vacancy

*"The trouble with recruitment and selection is that they are often unplanned. Organisations just respond as needs arise."*
Investors in People Recruitment and Selection Model (2002).

In a planned approach to recruitment, every vacancy should be used as an opportunity to undertake a thorough, forward-looking, review of the job. Considerations will include:

- Is there a clear business need for the role? Does the post need to be filled (or created, in the case of expansion)? Can the role be absorbed by the remaining employees in the section?
- Does the role need to be redefined in order to take account of changing business needs?
- Is it more appropriate to contract out to a supplier?
- Is there a possibility of pooling or sharing staff between organisations?
- If the vacancy is to be filled, on what basis? (eg full or part-time, permanent or fixed-term)

- Does the way the service is provided need to change? Information gleaned from customer feedback may be useful.
- Can elements of the post be mechanised?
- What skills/competencies are needed? (see below) Do the skills exist, or potentially exist, in-house?
- If the role is one with high turnover, consider whether the job can be made more interesting eg given more variety or greater responsibility (see Chapter 11).
- Is there the opportunity to work flexibly, in terms of hours or location? This may open up the role to people who otherwise would not consider it.

Information gleaned from exit interviews or consultation with the current jobholder and colleagues may well produce good ideas about useful changes to the role.

· · · · · · · · · · · · · · · · · · · · · · · · · · · · · · · · · · · · · · · · · · · · · · · · · · · · · · · · · · · · · ·

### Portsmouth City Housing Service

As part of a complete review of HR, the Housing Service identified an ad hoc and reactive approach to filling vacancies. Following reorganisation, the Council now employs dedicated recruitment officers, who work with line managers to plan for recruitment. For each vacancy there is a review of the current and future requirements for the role and the job description and person specification are updated to ensure they reflect the required competencies. The recruitment officers have also assisted in removing some unnecessary barriers to recruitment, and line managers have been trained in use of competencies and effective selection techniques.

· · · · · · · · · · · · · · · · · · · · · · · · · · · · · · · · · · · · · · · · · · · · · · · · · · · · · · · · · · · · · ·
· · · · · · · · · · · · · · · · · · · · · · · · · · · · · · · · · · · · · · · · · · · · · · · · · · · · · · · · · · · · · ·

### Cymdeithas Tai Clwyd and Cymdeithas Tai Eryri

Cymdeithas Tai Clwyd and Cymdeithas Tai Eryri are rural housing associations which currently share staff in both internal audit and best value reviews. The two organisations operate in adjoining local authority areas in North Wales. The arrangement works as the organisations both share similar values and practices eg conducting their business in Welsh. As well as being cost-effective, the initiative contributes to benchmarking and performance improvement.

· · · · · · · · · · · · · · · · · · · · · · · · · · · · · · · · · · · · · · · · · · · · · · · · · · · · · · · · · · · · · ·

## ❏ 6.2 Defining the role and candidate type

The CIPD (1998) states that *"successful recruitment depends on finding people with the necessary skills, expertise and qualifications to deliver organisational objectives and the ability to make a positive contribution to the values and aims of the organisation"*.

The first step in achieving this goal is identifying what the vacant role entails and what skills, competencies, knowledge and experience candidates will be expected to possess. Traditionally, organisations have produced job descriptions and personal specifications for this purpose. The approach involves breaking the job down into its component parts and working out which are the key objectives. A person specification listing the key attributes required to undertake the role can then be derived from the job description and used in recruiting the new person.

An alternative approach, which allows for greater flexibility, is to adopt a competency-based approach to recruitment.

## ■ Competencies and competency frameworks

The move to a competency-based approach has been a significant development in HR practice in recent years. It is seen as a means of achieving integration of human resource practices. Once a competency framework has been designed, it can be used in recruitment, selection, training and development, performance management and reward.

The competency approach has developed in response to the rapid pace of change facing most organisations, and the recognition that there is an increasing need to employ flexible people who match the wider context of working within the organisation. Less emphasis is placed on qualifications and rigid experience in a role, and transferable/portable qualities take on a greater significance. These will include, for example, fitting in with the organisation's values and having the necessary team and customer focus.

'Competency' is generally defined as the behaviours that an employee must have, or must acquire, to *input* into their work, in order to achieve high levels of performance. 'Competence' is a description of a work task or job *output*. Organisations commonly use a mixture of both tasks and behaviours as indicators within a competency-based approach.

When developing a competency approach, most organisations develop a competency framework. Typically, competency frameworks contain a mix of measurable behaviours, skills and knowledge. The framework will contain definitions or descriptions (known as behavioural indicators) that indicate how an individual can demonstrate that they meet the competency.

There are several models of competency framework:
- One framework for all employees across an organisation. This is often known as a 'core framework'.
- A core framework, supplemented by role specific competencies.
- A menu-style approach, whereby a few competencies are selected which are relevant to the role an individual performs.
- Different frameworks for different groups of staff (either based on function or on responsibility).

Both the CIPD and the Employers' Organisation for Local Government provide guidance on developing a competency framework and identifying actual competencies. The recommended approach is usually to adapt an existing model (that has been tried and tested) to the circumstances/culture of the organisation concerned. The following points are essential for successful implementation:

- Carry out research amongst employees and managers to use their knowledge in developing the competency headings and the indicators of performance
- Train managers on the practicalities of using the framework
- Provide information to all employees on the new framework and how it will be used

## ■ Identifying competencies for recruitment purposes

The principles of job descriptions and person specifications still apply when using a competency-based approach. However, it is necessary to break down what would traditionally be described as the job tasks, outputs, skills and experience, into competencies and behavioural indicators. The emphasis is thus on the attitudes, values and behaviours required instead of the skills and experience used traditionally. The resulting profile then indicates what will be required of the successful applicant for them to perform effectively within the job.

Profiles can focus exclusively on the current demands of the job or on how those requirements might alter in the future. In addition, competency profiles allow organisations to put greater emphasis on 'recruiting for potential' by looking for attitude and future ability.

It is important that competencies are reviewed periodically to ensure that they are still relevant and so that managers can think carefully about what they are looking for in the recruitment (and performance review) process.

## ■ Advantages of a competency-approach to recruitment

- It provides greater clarity for both the applicant and employer about what is required. For example, a person specification may state rather vaguely that 'initiative' is required. In a competency approach, behavioural indicators may include, *'is proactive in taking responsibility for everyday problems'* and *'does not wait for direction'*.
- By identifying broader attributes, it enables organisations to recruit from outside of their typical 'pool' (ie they are not limited to people with certain qualifications or experience). This is important for organisations wishing to increase the diversity of their staff.
- Setting out the required competencies encourages self-selection by potential candidates (see Chapter 8).
- Assists in determining the most appropriate method(s) of assessment (see Chapter 8).
- Time spent accurately identifying competencies at recruitment stage provides the basis for use of the competencies in future employment.

■ **Possible disadvantages**

- A competency approach can be extremely resource-intensive and may require external expertise.
- A critical aspect of all competency approaches is the level of detail. If too general, insufficient clarity will be provided. If too detailed, the entire process becomes over-complex, time-consuming and may lose credibility.
- Smaller organisations may find it difficult to go down the full competency route. However, they should find it possible to develop a halfway measure – a more structured approach to their job descriptions and personal specifications and one that concentrates on competencies and transferable skills, rather than task-based duties and experience.

## Bromford Housing Group

Bromford HG has a policy of recruiting externally at entry level, and promoting internally where possible.

At entry level, rather than focusing on housing experience and qualifications, the Group focuses on potential and the needs of the business. They place emphasis on values, a 'can do' attitude, customer focus, team working and self-confidence.

Skills frameworks are in place, describing expected behaviours and competency indicators. Managers are trained to carry out competency/behaviour interviews to identify these qualities during the selection process. The skills frameworks are also the foundation stones of the Group's approach to career and succession planning (see Chapter 11).

## Genesis Housing Group

Genesis HG was experiencing difficulties in recruiting to a large number of vacancies for Rent Recovery Officers. The original role requirements narrowed the post to those already working in the housing sector. However, a review of the requirements determined that the Group was actually looking for individuals with a financial background, who could follow policies and procedures and who could ultimately take tough action if required. It was recognised that specialist knowledge, such as a sound understanding of housing and welfare benefits, could be taught via training. The role profile was changed to reflect these basic requirements.

An advertising concept was agreed, working with Bartlett Scott Edgar Ltd recruitment advertising agency, which emphasised both the positives of the role and the need for hard decisions. The advertisements specifically mentioned other sectors where applicants might currently be working (eg bank or building society).

→

The advertisements, placed in the national and regional press, attracted 500 applicants mainly from the financial sector. 100 were long-listed and occupational skills tests (concentrating on the three key competencies of decision-making, technical checking and numerical assessment) were used as a means of producing a shortlist for interview. 15 candidates were invited to a panel interview, and eight appointments were made.

## Circle 33 Housing Trust

Circle 33 has a Customer Contact (Call) Centre providing management and maintenance services to tenants across London. This structure requires customer-focused staff who possess the knowledge and judgement to resolve problems at the point of the tenant's call.

The need to recruit staff who can demonstrate the required level of customer service skills is clearly addressed in the competency profiles and behavioural indicators for the role. The Trust does not ask for housing experience, taking the view that knowledge and experience can be most easily developed. They advertise in the local and BME press stressing the need for excellent customer service skills as a prerequisite to the post. Their advertisements highlight training and career opportunities, as well as the desire to recruit staff who are representative of the tenant base.

Their advertisements have resulted in over 1,000 applications each time. The Trust have outsourced the first stage of the selection process to a call centre, who carry out telephone interviews. They have developed an in-house assessment centre (see Chapter 8) for the second stage, where they take a holistic approach to identifying whether someone can/has the potential to demonstrate the desired qualities for the role.

The Trust has a four-week training induction programme, where the new recruits receive off-the-job training. The trainees' formal probationary period does not commence until they have passed skills and knowledge tests.

The Trust considers that the benefits of their approach far outweigh the substantial investment in recruitment, selection, off-the-job training and ongoing development. They report success on several counts:
- Appointment of high quality, diverse front-line staff with the potential to become future customer service managers
- Increased appointments from BME communities, including staff with key language skills
- Improved customer satisfaction.

## Denbighshire County Council

The experience of the housing rents team was discussed in more detail in Chapter 3. As one way of addressing the high turnover, Denbighshire CC recognised that it needed to change its recruitment profile, in order to attract new applicants and increase diversity amongst staff. Traditionally, the Council had considered housing experience as a requirement for the job, resulting in a narrow recruitment field. The emphasis was changed to look for people with portable skills, especially those who could demonstrate good customer awareness. The Council undertook to train them to ensure they had the necessary knowledge to do the job.

The team has successfully recruited people from retail, call centre staff and a training officer. They have found bringing in staff from a variety of backgrounds has introduced fresh ideas and impetus to the team, enabling them to develop new service initiatives.

# CHAPTER 7

## RECRUITMENT TOOLS

This chapter considers firstly the increasing trend to outsource some or all of the recruitment function. It then explores the expanding range of recruitment tools available to organisations, including:

- Media advertising
- Web-based recruitment
- Candidates' database
- Informal schemes (staff referral schemes, rehiring former employees)

## ❑ 7.1 Introduction

The aim of any recruitment process is to fill a vacant position with the best candidate, cost effectively and on time. The range of recruitment tools available to employers is expanding and the choice of method should depend upon the nature of the post to be filled. Targeting both the recruitment method, and the media used, to the post in question, will help employers to minimise costs. This approach should also ensure the organisation is not restricting the range of applications by always recruiting through the same channels.

## ❑ 7.2 Outsourcing recruitment and selection

Outsourcing recruitment and selection to external organisations is increasing and expected to accelerate. Research in 2001 by HR consultancy Cubiks, forecasts that employers will increasingly rely on niche providers to supply recruitment and other HR services, leaving in-house professionals to focus on business strategy.

External agencies and consultants can provide the following services:

- Draft and design advertisements or campaigns and arrange for adverts to be placed in suitable media
- Supply details of candidates held on their records, usually to fill short-term vacancies and may specialise in one particular occupation

- Find candidates by advertising on behalf of the organisation, assessing the response and providing the organisation with a shortlist
- Approach candidates from their own network of contacts (headhunting)

The recruitment process can be contracted out partly or wholly:

- For all posts or just for specific vacancies, or
- Different parts of the process can be outsourced eg the design and placement of advertisements.

## ■ Circumstances where outsourcing may be appropriate

- Where there is a skill shortage and competition is intense, it may be difficult to recruit without the aid of a third party.
- Where the in-house HR function does not have sufficient or appropriate resources eg to fill a large number of vacancies effectively or to recruit to an unfamiliar area.
- Where an organisation has a poor image, a dedicated advertising/ recruitment company may market the organisation more successfully.
- Outsourcing can be cost effective as employers benefit from economies of scale eg from lower advertising rates charged by press to agencies.
- Improved service may result from the service level agreement agreed with the agency.
- Filling permanent vacancies with temporary employees can reduce the urgency in filling posts, so giving the organisation more time to find the right person.
- On occasion employees may be offered a permanent post following a period of temporary employment. This can allow both the organisation and employee to assess suitability.

## ■ Possible disadvantages

- It can be expensive. The cost of a recruitment consultant can amount to a third of the advertised salary for the job in question. The cost of temporary workers can be double the rate paid to regular employees.
- Agency shortlists can be short, often only three or four candidates, emphasising the importance of providing full information (see below).
- It can be difficult for an intermediary to understand the business (eg in terms of ethos and values) and to judge an individual's ability to fit into an organisation.
- There is a danger that agencies may oversell the job when seeking to attract applicants.

**Good practice checklist:**
**Commissioning external advertising/recruitment services**

✓ Carry out a cost/benefit analysis.

✓ Consider impact on current service delivery and on those who currently undertake recruitment tasks.

✓ Examine the market carefully before selecting an agency. It is important to select an agency which has experience of the particular labour market and one which reflects the organisation's culture.

✓ Explore the agency's ability to comply with equalities legislation, its experience in promoting diversity and its track record in promoting diversity within its own workforce.

✓ Ask whether the agency belongs to a professional body (eg Recruitment and Employment Confederation, Management Consultancies Association). If so, request a copy of the professional code of conduct. If not, ask what quality procedures are in place and how client disputes are resolved.

✓ Ensure the Terms of Business have been carefully scrutinised and that the fee structure is transparent.

✓ Ask about the agency's level of success/details of their current performance.

✓ Speak to current or recent past clients (ask them to provide names).

✓ Be clear about what is required of the agency (eg the requirement to put out realistic recruitment messages). Provide a full, up-to-date brief in writing and ensure that any supporting information about the organisation is accurate.

✓ Have a written service agreement, outlining the responsibilities of each party (eg who is responsible for handling references).

✓ Be clear about how information will be shared between parties, ensuring compliance with data protection requirements.

✓ Agree which recruitment and selection tools will be used and ensure these are consistent with the organisation's recruitment policy. Where testing is to be carried out, check the consultants are appropriately qualified.

✓ Ensure arrangements are in place for effective monitoring of performance and review.

✓ Retain ownership via an exit strategy or other mechanism, eg agree an evaluation of the service at the end of year one.

## North Wales Housing Association

Following a comprehensive service review of HR, the association made a decision to outsource:

- Recruitment and selection (extent of service varying with the type of post)
- Employment relations/legal matters
- HR strategy development

Following tender, Insight HR & Management Consultants were appointed. The revised arrangements have enabled the association to reduce their HR staffing complement at a saving of £44,000 pa. They report that the initiative has been extremely successful, resulting in more professional advertising and modernised recruitment/selection processes.

## Hertfordshire County Council

Hertfordshire CC has outsourced its recruitment processes, including 2,700 job advertisements and 300,000 hours of temporary placements each year to a single agency, Manpower. Making full use of information technology and online recruitment, Manpower aims to improve recruitment standards while cutting costs by 5% over the life of the five year contract.

## ■ Executive search (head-hunting)

Organisations should weigh up the potential benefits and drawbacks of executive search/head-hunting particularly carefully before using it as a recruitment tool for any post. To maximise the benefits of the process, there are elements to build in to selecting and appointing an agency to ensure the organisation's needs are met.

Head-hunting can potentially be discriminatory. Candidates outside the consultant's network may be excluded, and where this occurs there is evidence that it tends to favour white males. To avoid possible discrimination, it is essential that head-hunting is carried out in an ethical way and organisations should establish what methods the agency has in place to avoid possible discrimination and reliance on the 'old boy' network.

- Ideally, head-hunting should only be used following unsuccessful open recruitment, unless it can clearly be demonstrated that the skills required are not available.
- Head-hunting must be a market exercise, identifying key players with relevant skills and experience. Consultants should be able to present information both for progressing strong candidates but also in order to reject weaker ones.

- Organisations must ensure agencies are using databases of good, but unsuccessful, candidates who they have previously interviewed and assessed (ie rather than including individuals on the strength of them seeming to be good).
- Organisations should only accept onto a shortlist candidates supported by interview reports and assessments outlining their specific suitability to the post in question.

Head-hunting might be an appropriate option where:

- Quality candidates are at a premium
- There is a particular niche area where skills are in very short supply
- There is a desire to bring in ideas from the commercial sector
- The role is critical to the success of the business and appointing the wrong person could be disastrous

It is also a useful, if costly, way of comparing internal candidates to the best available skills in the open market. However, it is not a quick fix, with the period from starting the assignment to the candidate taking up post generally taking six to nine months. It is relatively expensive, with successful head-hunters commanding fees of 25-50% of the job's salary. Before commissioning the agency, organisations should qualify these terms clearly, eg is the fee based on basic salary or complete package? What constitutes the package? Is staged payment required?

## ■ Interim managers

The practice of bringing in outside executives on short-term assignments is becoming more common within the housing sector. It is especially useful where organisations need an 'agent of change' fast, where recruitment would be too slow and where consultants would not be hands-on enough.

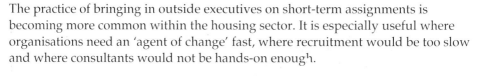

### HERA

HERA has developed a London-based scheme to identify and place high quality interim managers. Assessment and development days are run for interested candidates and a pool of assessed candidates is available for employers to select from.

## ❑ 7.3 Recruitment options

A brief summary of the main recruitment options is provided in the following table.

| Method | Advantages | Disadvantages | Most suited to |
|---|---|---|---|
| Job Centres | • Can produce applicants quickly<br>• Free service for employers<br>• Good means of tapping local market/supporting local communities<br>• Online recruitment site (Job Centre Plus) – can select from nationwide network<br>• Commitment to equal opportunity<br>• Disability Employment Advisers can provide advice on employing disabled people | • Registers are mainly of the unemployed – limits breadth of vacancies and type of people using the service<br>• Produces people for interview not genuinely interested in undertaking the job | Clerical or manual appointments |
| Notice boards and vacancy circulars | • Inexpensive<br>• Can be used internally and externally (eg supermarkets, libraries)<br>• Circulars can be used to promote organisational image and provide information to the local community | • Unsuitable for more senior or specialist staff | Clerical or manual appointments |
| Advertising in national newspapers | • Wide circulation<br>• First choice for most job seekers<br>• Attracts both active and passive job seekers<br>• Some national papers are accepted medium for certain posts, ie can reach a target audience<br>• Can help brand awareness and alter people's perceptions of an organisation | • Slow<br>• Expensive<br>• Much of cost wasted in reaching inappropriate people | Managerial, specialist, professional jobs<br>Graduates |
| Ethnic press | • Circulation amongst BME groups<br>• Sends positive diversity message | • Not available in all areas of UK<br>• Readership is limited | All posts |
| Trade journals | • Reaches a specific readership<br>• Accepted medium for certain posts, within the sector<br>• Attracts both active and passive job seekers, within the sector | • Readership is limited – may contribute to sector being seen as 'a club' | Specialist/ professional |

→

| Method | Advantages | Disadvantages | Most suited to |
|---|---|---|---|
| Local newspapers/ radio | • Likely to be read/heard by those seeking local employment<br>• Inexpensive – little wasted circulation | • Limited audience | Non-professional or technical jobs Young people |
| Web-based recruiting | • Large potential recruitment market<br>• Speed<br>• Cheaper than national press<br>• Provides up-to-date image<br>• Easy access to information by potential applicants<br>• Provides global coverage, 24 hours a day | • Can produce too many unwanted applications or none at all<br>• Is most effective when part of an integrated recruitment process – many organisations currently lack the resources/expertise for this. May require substantial investment in software/web design<br>• Can be viewed as impersonal<br>• Cannot rely solely on online recruitment as not all applicants have access – therefore additional cost of other methods.<br>• Monitoring of website traffic is less rigorous than distribution data for publications. Employers are less able to analyse the audience reached.<br>• Some evidence of unethical agencies (eg falsifying figures, using bogus CVs) | Graduates Increasingly, all types of posts |
| Candidate database | • Inexpensive<br>• Speed<br>• Useful where same post is recruited to frequently<br>• Low rejection rate as candidate already expressed an interest | • Small pool of suitable applicants | |
| Staff referral schemes | • Economical<br>• Can target scheme so that diversity is improved<br>• Links to higher rate of retention | • Small pool of suitable applicants<br>• Potentially unlawfully discriminatory where the work force is predominantly one sex or racial group (see below) | |

## Portsmouth City Housing Service

As one part of a wider review of its recruitment strategy, the Housing Service has been more innovative in the style and placement of advertisements.

Examples include:

- Setting up recruitment publicity stands at local community events
- Commissioning a city bus and 'wrapping' the outside in a Housing Service advertisement, with contact details for potential applicants.

## ■ Media advertising

### Good practice checklist: Use of media

✓ Effective advertising is a skill and many organisations will require specialist expertise (see checklist above on recruiting external agencies).

✓ To be effective, advertisements need to attract a good response from suitable candidates, discourage those who would be unsuitable and promote a positive image of the organisation.

✓ It is important to recognise that job advertisements may be the only publicity that many people see about the organisation. Their impact is wider than attracting someone to a specific job, and advertisements should aim to achieve positive recognition among potential applicants and existing and future stakeholders (see also Employer branding in Chapter 5).

✓ The correct choice of media is essential. Ask publications about their distribution and readership (eg occupation details).

✓ Consider timing both in terms of time of year and in ensuring cost effectiveness (eg by taking out one large advertisement with several posts). If timing allows, consider linkages with appropriate editorial or features.

✓ Be creative about where to look for people (eg target second career people leaving the commercial sector).

✓ Ensure compliance with anti-discrimination legislation (using advertisements to promote a more diverse workforce is addressed in Chapter 5).

## ■ Internet-based recruitment

(Note: use of the web for application and selection processes is discussed in Chapter 8).

### *Overview*

The use of the internet for recruitment purposes has grown massively in recent years, and will continue to increase as more people gain access to the internet. An e-recruitment study carried out by Workthing in 2003 found that 26% of the working population expects to get their next job online.

**Options for advertising online**

| | Advantages | Disadvantages |
|---|---|---|
| **Organisation's own website** Used by a higher proportion of organisations in the public sector, media and IT. | • Quick and inexpensive to set up <br> • Strong alignment with visitors <br> • Can capture visitors for other purposes <br> • Complements other channels <br> • Can contain much useful information – eg on career development, taster job profiles <br> • Can build exclusive talent pool <br> • Need not be the preserve of the largest organisations | • Good starting point but limited in approach, if website not visible and not used to full potential. Success is directly related to the number of people who visit the website. <br> • Optimising use of search engines/directories likely to need expert assistance, with cost implications. <br> • At best using online recruitment and cutting back on traditional advertising is likely to be cost neutral. |
| **Dedicated recruitment sites/job boards** Used by the retail, education and financial services. | • May attract many more potential applicants, especially if site is well known and focuses on relevant jobs <br> • Vacancies posted online are displayed almost instantaneously <br> • Organisations can be given protected access to the site, enabling them to publish, amend and remove jobs over the internet, 24 hours per day. <br> • Additional information about the organisation can be posted and links to own website can be incorporated <br> • Sites can provide a matching service between vacancies and CVs posted by job seekers | • More expensive – cost will depend on how high-profile the site is and on the organisation's presence on it. <br> • Employers can be restricted by lack of technical knowledge ie not using site to full potential. <br> • Huge job boards will only provide candidate with eg top 200 jobs – the organisation's job may never appear. <br> • Need to capture applicant quickly - they are likely to have applied for several jobs. |
| **Media sites** | • May attract more potential applicants than publication alone <br> • Can link with organisation's own website | • Expensive as the job will normally have to be advertised in the publication before being placed on the website. |

In terms of attracting applicants, the internet can be used by employers to:

- Advertise jobs on the organisation's own website
- Put background information for candidates on the organisation's website (eg on the careers available)
- Advertise on a dedicated recruitment site or job board
- Advertise on a media site (ie a website linked to traditional press advertising)
- Run their own candidate database by enabling potential candidates to register for email alerts of new vacancies
- Gain access to CVs filed by job seekers (candidate mining)

Small organisations might consider developing a local recruitment website in partnership with other organisations, for posting jobs.

### Where to advertise on the internet

The three main options for advertising online are summarised on page 72 opposite.

---

## Good practice checklist: Using the internet

**General**

✓ Consider whether the internet will be used just to advertise jobs or whether candidates will be able to apply online. For real cost and efficiency benefits to be apparent, everything should be done online.

✓ Consider what changes will be required to staffing responsibilities. What training and support will be needed?

✓ Consider how use of the internet as a recruitment source will be monitored.

✓ Ensure online advertisements make the most of the medium and do not just mirror print advertisements. Organisations may need specialist advice.

**Own website**

✓ Ensure the website address is promoted everywhere (eg development boards, publications) and that there is a prominent link from the website homepage to the jobs section.

✓ Take professional advice about optimising the use of search engines and directories and registering web addresses.

✓ Ensure site is well designed and easily navigated.

✓ Consider whether internet advertising will replace, or be used in addition to, more traditional forms of advertising. If used in addition, a prominent link directing people from the advert to the organisation's website, allows the size and cost of the advert to be reduced.

✓ If no current vacancies, make it clear when opportunities may emerge. Alternatively, invite people to register their details and alert by email when posts become available (see below).

→

---

**Job board sites**

✓ Carry out research before selecting a job board site. Canvass opinion and test sites before committing. Check whether sites attract a relevant audience (via job sites' own surveys).

✓ Ask sites for details of their performance. Request unique user data (ie number of different people visiting site over a specified period of time), not number of hits or average numbers of unique users. Are the figures independently audited?

✓ Consider different job sites for different jobs.

## Family Housing Group

Family HG have taken out striking advertisements in print, getting across key positive messages around diversity, customer focus and team working. The advertisements give only brief details of specific posts and instead direct people to their website, where full job details are given.

Family's website invites visitors to register their details, in order to be kept informed about what is happening at Family and suitable jobs.

## Network Housing Group

In response to the Group's difficulties in recruiting to the posts of Tenancy Services Officer (TSO) and Senior Tenancy Services Officer (STSO), People Media, the group's recruitment agency, set up a Candidate Mining (or Web Spider) programme.

Candidate Mining is a means of identifying and collecting suitable candidate CVs and data from the internet. The programme was set up, identifying key words from the TSO and STSO role profiles to use as search tools. The programme then used these key words to filter through hundreds of CVs already posted on internet job sites.

A total of 15 CVs for the two posts were presented to Network, who interviewed seven people. The candidates were exceptionally strong and the two posts were filled at a cost of £3000.

## ■ Candidate database

Also known as a candidate management system, this is basically a means of storing names of possible future candidates, either on paper file or computer database.

Names may come from a number of sources:

- Unsuccessful but suitable applicants who may be considered for future posts or vacancies elsewhere in the organisation. This can include internal as well as external applicants.
- People registering an interest on the website.
- Unsolicited enquiries.

In order to comply with data protection legislation, candidates must give their consent to their details being held. It is essential to check periodically that the individual wants to remain on the database, and details must not be passed to a third party. Organisations should stay in touch with the person, updating their details if their situation changes.

## Leeds City Council and Leeds ALMOs

Due to the frequency of vacancies amongst Clerk Cashiers within the ALMOs, the Council, which provides recruitment services on a service level agreement basis, keeps a database of suitable people who have been through the recruitment process for this post and who can be called upon when a vacancy arises.

## Graduate Opportunities for Local Government Database (GOLD)

GOLD is a free facility, provided by the Employers' Organisation for Local Government (EO), to enable local authorities to access a database of assessed graduates, interested in a career in local government. The graduates included in the database are those who have not quite met the requirements of the national graduate development programme for local government.

## ■ Informal recruitment

Informal recruitment measures include:

- Referrals from existing employees – employees are generally, but not always, offered a 'bounty payment' to put candidates forward who they believe would make successful recruits. Payment is made if the candidate is successfully appointed and remains in post for a period of time.
- Rehiring of former employees. In a sector where a large percentage of the workforce is female, women returning after career breaks will be an important group to target (examples of some initiatives enabling women to return to work are discussed in Chapter 13).

A major advantage of informal recruitment is its cost-efficiency. In addition, for both of the above categories of employees, there is evidence of higher retention and better performance in role. The reasons for this are likely to be:

- They have self-selected themselves in terms of suitability to the post.
- They have a good idea what to expect of the job and the organisation.
- In the case of staff-referral schemes, there is evidence of a higher quality of candidates, as people only tend to recommend acquaintances who they believe are suitable.

However, there are disadvantages to this type of approach:

- It is likely to produce only a small pool of suitable applicants.
- There may be a lack of diversity, with similar types of people being recruited from similar backgrounds.
- Where the workforce is predominantly one sex or racial group, employee referral schemes may be unlawfully discriminatory. The CRE recommends that *"employers should not recruit solely, or in the first instance, through the recommendations of existing employees where the workforce concerned is wholly or predominantly white or black and the labour market is multi-racial"*. Similarly, the EOC recommends that this practice should be avoided in a workforce predominantly of one sex. One means of addressing this is using schemes to enhance diversity, by making payment only where the candidate appointed is from an under-represented minority group.

Note: The evaluation of recruitment tools is addressed in Chapter 8.

# CHAPTER 8

# APPLICATION PROCESS
# AND SELECTION TOOLS

This chapter considers the need for many organisations to modernise elements of the application and selection process, particularly with a view to reducing bureaucracy and promoting a positive applicant experience.
It looks at the importance of encouraging self-selection, and examines some tools available to help employers to be rigorous in their selection process:

- Online screening
- Telephone screening
- Structured interviewing
- Testing
- Assessment centres

Finally, the need for formal evaluation of recruitment and selection processes is considered.

## ❑ 8.1 The need to modernise

### ■ A positive experience for applicants

The public sector is known for its cumbersome recruitment processes. Lengthy and bureaucratic recruitment procedures can put off applicants, not only because the process itself is slow but also because it may confirm an applicant's perception of what working in the sector might be like.

Application and selection processes in the housing sector are generally driven by a desire to be fair, and the balance between complying with equalities best practice and achieving an efficient recruitment process is a difficult one to achieve. However, there are ways in which bureaucracy can be reduced.

Organisations need to review their procedures and eliminate any unnecessary processes. The use of new technology (see below) will be an important consideration here. The key to reducing bureaucracy is to ensure that recruiting managers are properly trained and fully understand the legal framework, organisational aims and good practice in recruitment and selection. If this is in place, managers should be given the freedom to tailor overall procedures to suit the needs of their particular recruitment.

Projecting a favourable, modern image of the organisation throughout the recruitment and selection process is important. Failure to do so will colour the candidate's view in terms of what they could expect from the organisation as an employee. The underlying theme of the following measures is the need to improve professionalism and customer service:

- Offer a variety of ways of applying (see below).
- Respond quickly and professionally to enquiries to advertisements in order to maximise applications.
- 'Court' candidates, especially where there is a limited response to an advertisement (eg follow up initial enquiries; encourage the person to apply; remind them a few days before closing date; keep them informed of the process, and warn them about any delays).
- Ensure all recruitment material is targeted, relevant, up-to-date and sends out a consistent message.
- Offer the opportunity to discuss posts informally, ensuring the contact person is available and that calls are returned.
- Be flexible in offering dates, times and locations of interviews.
- Let people know what to expect (eg who will be on the interview panel).
- Avoid a one-sided process, by demonstrating what the organisation can offer the candidate.
- Ensure the needs of disabled applicants are addressed (eg send letters out with interview arrangements in sufficient time for any necessary arrangements to be made).
- It is good practice to let all candidates know the result of the recruitment process and to provide brief feedback if they ask for it. Send helpful rejection letters (eg where appropriate, candidates can be asked whether they would like to be considered for other posts and their name kept in a candidate pool (see Chapter 7).

•••••••••••••••••••••••••••••••••••••••••••••••••••••••••••••••••••••••••••••••••••

## Denbighshire County Council

Denbighshire CC was anxious to move away from the standard recruitment process of 'a boring advert and traditional half hour interview'. They were keen that the process genuinely demonstrated to applicants what working for the authority would be like and that it was very much a two-way process. Adverts are more dynamic and applicants now undertake a series of exercises directly related to the job, a short presentation and interview. At they end of the interview, the council invites candidates to say what their impression is of the authority.

•••••••••••••••••••••••••••••••••••••••••••••••••••••••••••••••••••••••••••••••••••

## Servite Houses

Servite Houses needed to minimise vacancies within Care Services. The positive action they have taken to retain existing staff is featured in Chapter 4. At the same time, they have sought to manage their recruitment differently in order to fill posts faster and more effectively:

- They have held Open Days for care staff, including on Saturdays. This process involves minimal form filling as the main information capture is done at interview. At the most recent event, 82 people were interviewed on the day and all vacancies filled. They have also used this to build up a growing relief pool, helped by their website.
- They have minimised the gap between closing date and interview, where they were losing potential staff.
- By inviting successful candidates in person, 48 hours after their interview, to complete Criminal Records Bureau (CRB) Disclosure forms with their new manager, they have been successful in reducing the time to administer this check by minimising mistakes/delays.

## Northern Ireland Housing Executive (NIHE)

Faced with the constant demand of filling clerical and other entry-level posts, the Housing Executive introduced 'Open Day Recruitment' sessions. Vacancies are advertised in advance and prospective candidates can complete application forms and attend interviews on the day. This initiative has proved:

- Cost effective as vacancies can be filled immediately
- An opportunity to promote working for the organisation, as other career opportunities are highlighted at the event.

## ■ Additional ways of applying – accepting CVs

The use of application forms in the housing sector has been widespread as a means of ensuring the same information is gleaned from each candidate. This sets a level playing field from an equalities point of view and helps to achieve consistency in the shortlisting process.

However, lengthy application forms are off-putting to some candidates. Many applicants prefer to provide a CV, which they can update quickly and use as an opportunity to sell themselves.

There are several disadvantages for employers accepting CVs:

- Shortlisting may be more difficult and less consistent
- Organisations may struggle to cope with the increased number of applications

- CVs often contain information that is irrelevant to the job
- There is greater potential for an applicant to be selective with the information given
- It is difficult to capture equal opportunities monitoring information

However, if organisations are serious about attracting a wider field of applicants, they need to adapt their processes to suit the needs and preferences of potential candidates. Organisations may wish to consider including guidance for applicants in the job pack, as to what information should be included in a CV.

····················································································

## Genesis Housing Group

A comprehensive review of the recruitment and selection service identified that the Group's application process was too rigid, and was deterring potential applicants in certain fields. As one step, the recruiting manager now determines whether CVs will be accepted from applicants in place of the traditional application form. This approach has proved successful, particularly in the functions of Finance, Marketing and HR and for management positions. To ensure that the standard declarations and equal opportunities information are provided, a basic form has been introduced to be completed and sent in with the individual's CV.

····················································································

## ■ Additional ways of applying – use of new technology

The use of online techniques to attract applicants has been discussed in Chapter 7. There is a variety of electronic techniques to continue the application and selection processes.

The simplest method is for organisations to accept email requests for job packs, which are then sent out manually.

Increasingly, organisations are providing all information relating to the job and the organisation online. The options here are:

- Enable application forms to be printed off and returned as hard copy.
- Accept completed application forms returned by email.
- Accept applications completed on your own website. These can be interactive forms, guiding candidates through each stage.
- Accept completed applications from a job-board internet site.
- Accept CVs by email or allow CVs to be automatically uploaded.
- Acknowledge the application online.
- Circulate applications electronically to appropriate managers for shortlisting.

*Advantages*

- Automation helps each step to be more effective and streamlined.
- Easing of administrative burden (less paper, less collation and posting of packs).
- Longer term cost benefits.
- Some systems can perform much of the initial screening of candidates (see below).

*Possible disadvantages*

- If technological advances are responded to in an ad hoc way, employers can find that their workload increases as a result of using electronic forms of recruitment/application. Mapping out processes is vital – it is not just about automating existing paper processes.
- Organisations can struggle to cope with the volume of applications.
- High drop-out rate among candidates filling in their online form, hence the need for easily navigable sites.

For the real cost and efficiency benefits to be apparent with online recruitment and selection, the entire process needs to be automated.

## ■ Seeking feedback from applicants

It is important to base any improvements to the recruitment process on the experiences of the people who use it (ie successful and unsuccessful candidates and recruiting managers). There are a number of ways of informing the process:

- Sending a questionnaire to unsuccessful applicants
- Asking unsuccessful applicants, when giving feedback, of their experience of the recruitment process
- Informal discussion with new recruits
- Asking managers how the process went
- Sending a questionnaire to those who requested job details but chose not to apply.

## ❑ 8.2 Encouraging self-selection

Self-selection is increasingly seen as an important means of improving the quality of candidates in terms of their suitability for vacancies. There is a fine balance to be struck between attempting to reduce rejection rates and early turnover whilst not letting those candidates that are genuinely appropriate to select themselves out of the running.

## ■ Realistic job previews

The need to give an honest impression of the job and organisation has been discussed in Chapter 5. It is important for organisations to be realistic about what they portray, and ensure they deliver what they have promised. Otherwise, new postholders' disappointment is likely to lead to poor performance and high turnover. Many employers are taking further steps to help potential candidates decide whether or not the job would suit them. Examples include:

- Providing brochures, videos or CD-Roms with further information.
- Offering an informal discussion with job holders.
- Inviting potential recruits to an open day.
- Inviting potential applicants to work alongside an existing employee for a shift. There is evidence that this has reduced early turnover in care homes, where new recruits had in the past been unprepared for the realities of the work.

### Llamau Housing and Support

Llamau held a combined AGM and Jobs Fair, with the aim of promoting the organisation's work to potential new staff as well as celebrating the past year. The event was widely publicised beforehand and was open to anyone who wanted to find out more about the organisation. Staff and service users were available to answer questions, so that people could hear at first hand what the work involves. Personnel staff had available application forms and job descriptions for current and likely future vacancies, and were able to advise people who had little experience of form-filling. In three hours, nearly 300 people attended the job fair; around 230 application forms were given out and around 160 returned, with many leading to new appointments. This was a period of expansion for Llamau, and the organisation was keen to maintain the existing diversity and commitment of their workforce. The jobs fair contributed to attracting new team members who share the organisation's values.

### Metropolitan Housing Trust (MHT)

MHT has held open days when recruiting to its Assisted Living Schemes for older people. The days enable potential recruits to see the schemes, talk to existing staff members, meet tenants and generally get a good idea of what the job would be like. Staff are also on hand to offer assistance with the completion of application forms.

## ■ Self-selection tests

A further way of encouraging applicants to select themselves into, or out of, the running for a job is by asking them to do some kind of self-selection questionnaire, included either with the application pack or on the website. Questions are about the candidate's previous work experiences and relate to the job for which they are applying. Candidates are advised that if they do not score over a certain level, it is unlikely they will be successful in their application.

### Audit Commission

The Audit Commission includes a two-page self-assessment questionnaire with its recruitment pack for the post of Housing Inspector, and encourages prospective applicants to complete it honestly. The questionnaire covers both previous experience and personal attributes. Typical statements include:

- *I am confident when making presentations to large audiences*
- *I do not have difficulties giving feedback ...even if the message is critical and the response is hostile*

For each of the key question areas there is a benchmark, and candidates are advised that if they do not match the benchmarks then the job is unlikely to be for them.

## ■ Competency-based approach

A competency-based approach to recruitment (see Chapter 6) can also help the individual to determine whether they match the competencies required to undertake the job, and the values of the organisation.

## ❑ 8.3 Selection tools

Increasingly, employers are going beyond qualifications and experience and exploring whether the candidate has the personal attributes and competencies to succeed in a role. There has been a considerable growth in use of selection methods that are believed to be better predictors of future performance.

There is a variety of methods available to help in the selection process. It is generally appropriate to use a range of methods, with the choice depending on:

- Type of post, what needs to be measured and accuracy required
- Staff skills available
- Administrative ease
- Budget
- Time factors

# ■ Screening/shortlisting applications

To ensure that shortlisting is done fairly, it must always be carried out by more than one person. Applicants must be scored systematically against the pre-determined role requirements. Changing criteria to enable someone to be included on the shortlist may be unlawful.

Some methods used by organisations to attract candidates may have the effect of significantly increasing the number of applications (eg web-based advertising and encouraging CVs). Organisations must have in place systems to allow applications to be filtered quickly, whilst ensuring they do not deselect potentially suitable candidates.

### Online screening

Online systems are available which filter applications automatically. This approach requires that all applications are received online and is therefore tied to web-based recruiting. Advocates of web-based recruiting point to this filtering of applicants as the crucial element in achieving cost savings by attracting applications through the internet.

A number of the packages available work by looking for key words or phrases, demonstrating particular qualifications, experience or competencies. Some also provide a scoring mechanism. Packages must be used alongside the skills of professional recruiters to ensure that the right criteria are used for selection. In addition, applicants must be informed if an automated shortlisting system is being used as the sole basis for making a decision.

### Advantages

- Speed, particularly where large numbers of applications are received
- Frees up staff time
- More consistent and objective decisions

### Disadvantages

- Success will depend on the recruiter's ability to select the appropriate key words and to provide enough detail in the job advertisement to ensure that suitable candidates respond appropriately.
- CVs may get longer as applicants strive to include every possible key word or phrase.
- Could be discriminatory for people who do not have English as a first language.
- Encourages conformity and may work against originality and the benefits of diversity.
- Possible perverse decisions relating to the IT package.

### *Outsourcing*

Outsourcing this element of the process is a further option where organisations are not geared up for a large number of applications. It is essential to provide clear and specific instructions to the agency.

## ■ Longer shortlists

Organisations experiencing difficulties in filling posts, may need to consider shortlisting differently. To ensure potential quality candidates are not being excluded, it may be appropriate to produce a long-list, whereby larger numbers are assessed at the first stage eg via shorter preliminary interviews or telephone interviewing.

### *Telephone interviewing*

Telephone interviewing is increasingly being used as a first stage selection tool, instead of preliminary interviews. Advantages include:

- Fast and inexpensive, so allowing a greater number of candidates to be considered.

- Useful if telephone skills are an important part of the job.

- Can help increase diversity by removing any bias on the part of the interviewer based on a candidate's appearance. There is evidence that telephone interviewing has helped to broaden the age range of new employees in organisations.

Possible difficulties include:

- Logistical difficulties of arranging the interview, especially if the candidate is already in employment

- Inflexibility eg the interview script may not allow further elaboration

The training of interviewers is crucial to success. Interviewers need to be skilful at eliciting the required information.

## ❑ 8.4 Interviews

Research amongst employers shows almost unanimous use of interviews and a strong belief that they are the most important tool in making selection decisions. Academic research reveals however that traditional selection interviews have poor predictive ability and are open to subjectivity and prejudice.

A survey of line managers carried out in 2003 showed that less than half felt they had adequate skills to select the right staff.

---

## Good practice checklist: Conducting interviews

✓ Highly structured interviews are considered much better at predicting future job performance. Advance preparation of relevant questions and their structuring is essential. Questions should focus on the attributes necessary to do the job and answers should be assessed against an agreed system.

✓ Behavioural questions ie those that focus on the candidate's past to demonstrate the behaviours necessary in the post, tend to produce better results than hypothetical (what if...?) situation questions. It is harder to concoct answers to behavioural questions. Behavioural questions are most often used in competency-based interviews, to reflect the different dimensions of the job. For example, asking an applicant for a Neighbourhood Officer, "How do you handle difficult customers?" will get a hypothetical response. Alternatively, asking "Tell me about a difficult situation with a customer: what did you do? and what was the outcome?" should uncover whether they have the right skills in this area.

✓ Interviews must be carried out by a panel of trained individuals, who are able to judge the applicant's skills and competencies. Training should combine the theory of behavioural interviewing with practical examples of technique (eg how to probe and ask follow-up questions) and the chance to put into practice the skills learned.

✓ Interviewers should receive regular refresher training. This is particularly true for senior managers, who may not be familiar with more recent techniques.

✓ Ensure training covers equalities legislation, the organisation's recruitment policy and general awareness training (eg guidance on the effects that generalised assumptions and prejudices can have on selection decisions).

✓ Consider the composition of the panel. Is it appropriate to involve trained tenants for relevant posts or to use staff panels for senior appointments to enable a wider perspective?

✓ Does the panel reflect diversity criteria? Organisations unable to resource this internally, might consider working in partnership with other organisations to achieve this.

✓ Interviews should be viewed as a two-way process – to find out if the candidate is suitable and to give them information about the job and the organisation. It is important that mutual expectations are explored and that the candidate has every opportunity to ask questions.

✓ If possible, show candidates where they would be working and introduce them to future colleagues.

✓ The length and style of the interview should be tailored to the job and the organisation. Structured interviews need not be formal.

✓ Ensure each candidate is given the same opportunity to present themselves.

✓ Consider whether any adjustments need to be made to accommodate an interviewee who has indicated a disability, or other special requirement, on the application form (eg talking through pre-selection information with a visually impaired candidate).

✓ Papers and notes should be retained for six months after interviews.

Further guidance on conducting interviews is produced by ACAS.

# ❏ 8.5 Selection testing

Testing is used to obtain information about a candidate, which would be difficult to obtain through the interview process. Advocates of testing point to the accuracy and objectivity of test data. Tests can be seen as giving credibility to selection decisions, so increasing confidence that the right person has been appointed.

## ■ Types of test for occupational use

### *Practical tests/attainment tests*

If the job involves practical skills, it may be appropriate to test at the time of interview eg typing or basic numeracy or literacy tests.

••••••••••••••••••••••••••••••••••••••••••••••••••••••••••••••••••••••

### Canmore Housing Association

Canmore HA felt the most apt practical test for the recruitment of a Property Services Assistant would be dealing with maintenance issues over the telephone. They employed an occupational psychologist to design a telephone test, in liaison with HR. The test was very useful in distinguishing between candidates who had scored similarly in the interview.

••••••••••••••••••••••••••••••••••••••••••••••••••••••••••••••••••••••

### *Aptitude tests*

These tests measure mental ability (generally through testing maths, verbal reasoning and logic) and enable employers to predict how an individual will perform in the job. These tests have right and wrong answers. Candidate's scores are compared against a predetermined 'norm' (ie against the scores of a normal population of similar people). Providing the test accurately reflects the requirements of the job, the process can add much to the validity and reliability of the selection decision.

However, such tests are not without difficulty:

*   Practical intelligence, associated with success in organisations, may be different from the nature of intelligence measured by tests.
*   Ability tests are really only a guide to education and should be used sparingly. A decision should never be based solely on such tests.
*   It is essential that the norm groups used are tested for their relevance to the workforce. There is some evidence that ability tests are potentially discriminatory to BME candidates, especially where English is not the first language. There is an option to use different norm groups to avoid this problem (see Circle 33 good practice example on page 89).
*   There is some evidence that ability tests are potentially discriminatory to disabled candidates. It is possible to change test conditions eg extend time allowed for disabled people.

### *Personality tests*

Personality questions are a systematic way of the candidate describing themselves through their responses to a questionnaire. The test might show, for example, whether someone is primarily concerned with social or financial issues. The intention is that such tests should not be used in a judgemental way, but should be used to stimulate discussion with the candidate. Results are generally validated though an interview with the applicant and together the results are used to predict behaviour in the particular job context.

A well-designed, professionally administered questionnaire can add validity to the selection process as it can predict future performance reasonably accurately. It can identify emotional or personality issues that would not arise at interview.

However, the use of these tests is controversial for a number of reasons:

- They assume there is an ideal personality for a particular job, which could lead to a lack of diversity

- They rely on the individual's willingness to be honest, because although there are no right and wrong answers, the best answer in terms of the job may be easy to pick out

- Training and experience are likely to have a greater impact on job performance than personality

Note: the generic terms 'psychological', 'occupational' or 'psychometric testing' are all largely used interchangeably to cover aptitude tests and personality tests.

---

### Good practice checklist: Using selection tests

✓ In deciding whether to use selection testing, consideration must be given to the objectives of the exercise, the nature of the vacancy, the number and type of candidates, the costs and the likely benefits.

✓ Tests need to be selected, used, interpreted and results fed back, by trained or qualified testers. Organisations may choose to train staff internally to administer the tests or to outsource this process. The former will be much more cost effective for organisations with an ongoing need.

✓ There are a multitude of tests available. It is essential to be clear what is being tested for, to enable the right test to be selected. Any testing must relate to the necessary requirements of the job. Organisations should ensure they receive evidence from the test suppliers on the following issues:
  - the reliability of the test and its consistency as a measure
  - the validity of the test
  - that the test has been used effectively in similar circumstances
  - that the tests do not unfairly disadvantage certain groups
  - that the norm groups are up to date and appropriate for the organisation's requirements. Do the norm results apply to a sufficiently representative mix of occupations, gender or ethnic groups to allow fair comparison with the user's group?

→

✓ Test scores need to be evaluated in the context of other information about the individual and should not be used as the sole selection technique. Organisations should be aware that where a decision is made solely on the automatic processing of personal data, an applicant may require, under the Data Protection Act 1998, that the organisation reconsiders any rejection or makes a new decision on another basis.

✓ Record sheets must be retained in accordance with data protection legislation.

✓ Applicants should be advised prior to attending for interview that testing will be used. It is good practice to provide a sample of the test they will encounter. They must understand how the test information will be used in the decision-making process.

✓ Candidates should be offered feedback on their performance.

✓ Test use should be monitored continuously to ensure that it does not discriminate, that it remains appropriate to the purpose and that norms are up to date and relevant.

Property People Publications has produced a review of psychometric testing for the housing sector. Details and sources of further guidance on testing are contained in Appendix 2.

## Circle 33 Housing Group

Circle 33 has used assessment centres, encompassing a range of tests, interviews, group exercises and presentations, since 1995. They have highly trained staff who carry out all aspects of the assessments in-house. Assessors come from across the organisation, not just HR and, in their experience, managers have been pleased to develop these new skills.

Assessors measure candidates against the agreed competencies for the post. Their intention is for appointments to be made on potential as well as experience, so enabling the appointment of staff who can progress within the organisation. Circle 33 believes the set-up costs, in terms of training staff and buying test materials, is more than outweighed by the benefits of successful recruitment, including reduced turnover in the first months, and through their ability to promote internally.

Conscious of the concern over possible gender, culture and disability bias in the use of psychometric testing, tests are never used in isolation and test results are always balanced against a raft of other evidence from the assessment day. The Group has established their own norm groups for the main tests that they use, drawing on the results of tests taken by many applicants to the association over the years. This ensures that the comparative group includes the full gender and ethnic mix of people who have applied for jobs with Circle 33 (rather then from the wider population). →

The Group reports that in the last year, for all internal and external recruitment (for which some form of psychometric testing would always be used), 55% of appointees were from BME groups and 60% were female, suggesting that including such tests within their recruitment framework has not had an adverse impact in relation to gender or cultural issues.

........................................................................................................

## ■ Online psychometric testing

Online psychometric testing is available 'off the shelf'. However, there are several problems associated with monitoring such tests. For example, it is difficult to guarantee that the test is being completed by the candidate and also that it is being completed within a standard, pre-determined time limit.

## ❏ 8.6 Assessment centres

Assessment centres evaluate individuals using multiple exercises to simulate elements of the job. An assessment centre need not be a physical site, but rather describes a process, whereby exercises, individual and group, take place over a day or a few days. Typical exercises include: role-playing, leaderless group discussions, in-tray exercises, tests, interview and presentation.

Organisations can outsource the running of assessment centres or can hold assessment days in-house. Whether or not the assessment centre is outsourced, it should reflect the reality of the job and the organisation.

Assessment centres are recognised as one of the most effective methods of selection and assessing potential because evaluation is based on direct observation. Research has shown that well-designed centres with a variety of activities can reach 0.8 predictive validity in assessing future performance (where 1.0 is perfect prediction).

However, they are costly to establish and administer, hence the tendency to use them for manager and graduate appointments. The cost needs to be weighed against the high predictive validity and the potential costs of recruitment error with other selection techniques. Smaller organisations might consider pooling assessment expertise between a number of organisations.

---

**Good practice checklist: Assessment centres**

✓ Design considerations will include: duration; location; candidate numbers and backgrounds; and the number, mix and experience of assessors.

✓ The current, and likely future, job skills and competencies must be determined at the outset. Tasks and tests must then be selected to match these.

✓ The day must appear fair, in terms of the tasks set and opportunities for candidates to demonstrate different aspects of their abilities.

→

---

✓ Consider the balance between tasks which encourage competitiveness, and those that encourage co-operation. Organisations wishing to improve diversity should increase opportunities for candidates to co-operate, as these skills are likely to encourage wider participation.

✓ Consider how feedback will be given.

Aside from the cost, the main drawbacks of assessment centres are specific to the type of exercises candidates are asked to perform (see table below).

| | Advantages | Disadvantages |
|---|---|---|
| Role play | • Assessor gets a chance to see how a candidate reacts in a realistic scenario<br>• Candidate gets a feel for type of work they will be doing | • Some job content does not lend itself to role play |
| Leaderless group discussions<br>Candidates asked to discuss a topic whilst being observed | • Assessors can judge how candidates interact and their communication and leadership skills | • Can generate a competitive environment<br>• Every group will differ depending on make-up so selection decisions could be unfair |
| In-tray exercises | • Can test a number of different competencies: eg decisiveness, problem solving, organisational skills<br>• Candidate gets a feel for type of work will be doing | • Poor construction of the in-tray will make this approach ineffective |
| Unseen written case study<br>Candidates asked to compose briefing note and report back verbally to interview panel | • Tests knowledge, ability to compose concise briefing note under pressure and get key points across. | • Not relevant to all job content |
| Presentations/ briefings<br>Applicant is given a topic and a timeframe to deliver a presentation | • Tests whether candidates can develop reasoned and succinct arguments<br>• Useful if the job will require this skill | • Candidates can get very nervous |

# ❑ 8.7 Employment checks

The employment checks that a local authority or housing association may need to undertake will include:

- References
- Eligibility to work
- Medical checks
- Criminal records

Ideally employment checks should only be carried out once the person has been selected. This will involve less administration and help prevent breaches of data protection or human rights legislation.

## ■ References

Obtaining references allows verification of the accuracy of statements made by the applicant and may provide an opinion on their suitability for the post. It is good practice to ask for evidence of the candidate's ability to meet the specific job requirements, rather than asking for a general character reference. The potential employee's permission must be obtained prior to contacting referees.

The process of obtaining references is a common cause of delay in the recruitment process. Organisations should consider taking up references by telephone, using a pro-forma questionnaire and keeping a record of the salient points. If using written references, sending a pro-forma will aid completion and prompt return.

## ■ Eligibility to work

Before making an appointment, employers must check the candidate's eligibility to work in the UK, under the Asylum and Immigration Act 1996. The Government has introduced changes, effective from 1 May 2004, to the types of document employers need to check to avoid employing illegal workers.

It is essential not to make assumptions about candidates as this might amount to discrimination. A Home Office Code of Practice is available giving advice on types of checks and how to avoid possible racial discrimination when meeting the obligations imposed by the Act.

## ■ Medical checks

There are important issues under disability, data protection and human rights legislation that employers need to consider with regard to medical checks. Comprehensive guidance is available from the Employers' Organisation.

## ■ Criminal records

A brief summary of the provisions of the Rehabilitation of Offenders Act 1974, in relation to checking criminal records, is provided in Appendix 1. Since March 2002, the system of checking records (disclosures) has been available through the Criminal Records Bureau (CRB). The CRB has produced a Code of Practice for organisations dealing with disclosures.

## ❏ 8.8 Evaluation of recruitment and selection processes

It is vital to identify the recruitment and selection techniques that provide the best results, in terms of quality candidates, for the lowest cost. This process requires formal evaluation. Organisations need to consider whether:

- Recruitment practices yield enough suitable candidates to enable the organisation to select sufficient numbers of high-calibre employees (effectiveness)

- A sufficient pool of candidates could be attracted using less expensive methods (efficiency)

- The recruitment methods are fulfilling the organisation's equal opportunities and diversity responsibilities (fairness)

Measures will include (for each recruitment/selection technique or medium used, as appropriate):

- Number of initial enquiries
- Number and quality of completed applications
- Number of successful appointments
- Number of vacancies re-advertised
- Turnover (numbers of recruits leaving, eg within six months, one or two years)
- Performance of individual within the job (eg either via performance indicators or feedback by new recruit's manager)
- Equal opportunities monitoring at each stage of the process to determine whether the equal opportunities/diversity policy is working (see Chapter 5 and sources of further guidance in the final section)

Evaluation of the recruitment and selection process from the point of view of the applicant has been discussed earlier in this chapter.

# CHAPTER 9

# 'GROWING YOUR OWN' TRAINEE SCHEMES

This chapter looks at the increasing trend for organisations to address their recruitment difficulties by 'growing their own' staff through:

- Trainee schemes
- Modern Apprenticeships
- Graduate recruitment and graduate development schemes

## ❏ 9.1 Introduction

Earlier chapters have explored how housing organisations can no longer rely, both in terms of numbers and of the skills and attributes required, on recruiting from the existing pool of experienced housing staff. Structured training schemes are essential for ensuring that recruits from outside the sector quickly acquire the necessary housing-specific skills and knowledge. In addition to recruiting from other sectors to fill the gap, many organisations are choosing to develop their own employees 'from scratch' through structured training schemes.

Such schemes are an important way for organisations to attract, develop and maximise the potential of individuals. This recruitment solution involves taking a longer-term perspective, whereby staff with the right attributes are 'nurtured' to fill the roles in question.

## ❏ 9.2 In-house trainee schemes

Many housing organisations have been active in this area and the good practice examples below show a variety of approaches.

## Advantages

- Staff are developed to suit the individual needs of the organisation
- The organisation potentially gets more from its initial investment in the employee, in the course of two or three roles, rather than just the initial vacancy filled
- Such schemes can improve diversity, as applications are not restricted by the requirement for certain qualifications/experience.

## Disadvantages

- Schemes require a substantial investment in training
- More intensive line management is required, putting greater pressure on existing staff
- Trainee schemes are not an effective solution to short-term recruitment crises
- Schemes must be coupled with a rigorous retention strategy in terms of maximising opportunities for development, planned career paths and support to study.

## Broadway

Broadway, a charity for homeless people in London, has chosen to invest in people with potential in order to address its recruitment difficulties, rather than rely on traditional advertising.

There is a twice-yearly intake of people who demonstrate an aptitude for their work but do not have relevant experience. Trainees receive a year-long intensive programme of core skills and on-the-job training. Entry-level posts are ring-fenced for them.

Broadway cite the benefits of their approach as:
- Attracting particularly motivated recruits, with a freshness of approach
- Reduced turnover and absenteeism
- Increased diversity amongst the workforce
- Significantly improved service delivery.

## Genesis Housing Group

The Group launched its Trainee Housing Officer Scheme in 1997. Trainees are appointed at one grade lower than a Housing Officer and undertake a comprehensive 12-month training programme. Much of the training is on-the-job, supported by in-house training courses. Progress is monitored by continuous assessment over the 12-month period and is recorded in a training log. On successful completion of the programme, the trainees are confirmed in post as a 'full' Housing Officer, on the HO grade.

→

The scheme is open to both internal and external candidates. Externally, the scheme has been advertised in the media and through university career services to target recent graduates. In addition the scheme has been offered to housing undergraduates looking for year-long placements as part of their course.

The success of the initiative has led to it being extended to cover other posts, for example:

- Trainee Administrator (targeting school leavers and women returners to work)
- Trainee Gas Surveyor (two year training programme).

## Thames Valley Housing (TVH)

TVH was concerned about high staff turnover. Information from exit interviews and staff surveys showed dissatisfaction with training, which tended to be ad hoc, and a lack of opportunity for career progression. In response, TVH put in place a planned, structured training programme to foster a learning culture and to assist staff at several levels to maximise their potential.

Competency-based qualifications in customer care, housing and management were introduced to give a large number of staff the opportunity to improve their skills. To ensure that the qualifications became embedded in organisational culture, TVH was the first housing association to achieve accreditation to deliver NVQs in Housing at Level 2, 3 and 4. The association has also gained City & Guilds accreditation as an NVQ assessment centre. Accreditation ensures the long-term future of the programmes as TVH can offer the courses to delegates from other housing associations.

The organisation was committed to the principle of integrating training within the workplace. NVQs set national competency standards and candidates must demonstrate that they have used these skills in the workplace. TVH delivered the programmes through a combination of workshops, one-to-one assessment sessions and work-based projects. The projects related directly to organisational improvements (eg complaints management).

TVH reports considerable success in developing and retaining staff. Turnover reduced from 37% to 16% between 2001 and 2003 and flexibility has improved, with 12 internal promotions or lateral moves compared to two in the same period previously. The Association also reports increased success in recruitment due to the training opportunities on offer.

## Irish Centre Housing

In response to difficulties in recruiting experienced and motivated staff, Irish Centre Housing introduced the post of trainee project worker at a lower grade, putting the salary shortfall into additional training. Progression to 'full' project worker can take up to one year. Recruitment was targeted amongst service users and residents as well as people looking for a career move into social housing. The association reports they have been able to attract more motivated people, who have become some of the organisation's best staff.

## PATH National Limited

PATH is a national training organisation, which aims to provide training and work programmes targeted at people from ethnic minorities. With over 18 years experience PATH has trained more than 2000 men and women from BME communities for professional careers.

Initially the organisation focused on housing management but its programmes now cover a wide range of industries and sectors, including health, construction, finance and information technology. PATH National also runs Management Development Programmes for employers who wish to upskill their staff. The programmes are structured to meet the requirements of particular posts and may run for between one and three years. Training is provided through on-the-job experience with an employer, day release and complementary short courses to assist with personal development. Personal Advisors carry out reviews (every 6-8 weeks) to ensure that both trainee and employer are happy with the programme and that progress is being made.

Following training, the trainee secures employment in open competition on merit. The programmes have been highly successful, with 96% of those trained going on to full-time employment, or to further education, within four months of completing their course.

Two examples of PATH trainee programmes relating to housing are featured below.

## Rochdale Housing Initiative (RHI)

RHI (a partnership of housing associations, Rochdale MBC, private developers, funding institutions and the voluntary sector) has developed a Positive Action Training Scheme. The scheme is aimed at residents of Rochdale, from an Asian background, who are not in employment.

→

The scheme has two main aims:

- To improve the representation of Asian people in the workforce
- To address the difficulties in recruiting qualified and experienced staff, which was beginning to impact on ability to deliver a range of projects.

The traineeship lasts 12 months and trainees are placed in real jobs with a range of housing organisations, who provide onsite training via a pre-agreed training plan. The employer funds 50% of the cost of the trainee. Trainees attend a day-release housing course tailored to their background and appropriate to the job. Courses range from a BTEC in housing to a post graduate certificate.

Trainees are assisted at the end of the programme to find permanent work (eg assistance in making applications and with interview skills). The trainee scheme has grown from five to 26 trainees in two years, and there is a strong demand from both trainees and employers.

### Gwalia Housing Association

Gwalia HA currently supports one trainee on its PATH scheme. Under the scheme, Gwalia provides a work experience placement and supports the individual on a housing training course of their choice. The individual receives a training allowance (commensurate with a salary), course fees and expenses. The current trainee is studying for a two-year part-time CIH diploma in housing and in the third year will complete an MSc in housing. During their time with Gwalia they have worked in all parts of the organisation, so gaining a comprehensive overview of the organisation.

Gwalia consider the scheme has brought considerable benefits to the organisation as well as to the individual. They point to a greater appreciation by staff of the needs of the diverse communities of Swansea, and a growing confidence amongst various groups that they can access services provided by the organisation. The scheme is being extended to provide a second training opportunity in supported housing.

## 9.3 Modern Apprenticeships

Modern Apprenticeships are a further way for organisations to equip employees with the skills and experience they need. Schemes are delivered in partnership with a local training provider and the apprentices get hands-on experience and on-the-job training, and at the same time gain qualifications.

Organisations can either take on a young person aged 16-24 as an apprentice or develop existing staff by enrolling them onto the programme. Financial assistance is available towards the cost of training and assessment from the Learning and Skills Council. Apprenticeships normally last between one and three years and there are two levels: Foundation (FMA) and Advanced (AMA) at NVQ Levels 2 and 3 respectively. Housing Modern Apprenticeships are only available at Advanced Level.

Benefits to the organisation include:
- A means of tackling skills shortages in particular areas
- Apprentices gain skills training directly relevant to the sector/role, at little cost to the employer
- A means of addressing the imbalance in the age profile of the workforce
- All training, and monitoring and review procedures, are conducted on behalf of, and in conjunction, with the employer.

The employer's responsibilities include:
- Recruitment (although assistance is provided).
- Induction and on-the-job training.
- Paying apprentices in full-time employment. A salary is negotiated that reflects skills, experience, age, abilities and the going rate for the job.
- Giving apprentices enough time and resources for training and assessment commitments.
- Contributing to the regular review of the apprentice's progress.

## Ribble Valley Borough Council

The Borough Council employs modern apprentices on two, three and four-year fixed term contracts in the legal, financial, surveying, engineering, electrical, housing and IT sections. They receive the same benefits as permanent members of staff, including competitive salary, membership of the pension scheme and flexitime arrangements. Apprentices gain practical work experience whilst studying, on a day-release basis, towards nationally recognised qualifications. The council reports success in apprentices going on to achieve permanent positions within the authority.

## Pennine Housing 2000

The Association, through its *More than Bricks and Mortar* project, operates a Modern Apprenticeship scheme with Lovell and Keepmoat, its major contracting partners. Apprentices are employed by Lovell on a traineeship contract but work with any of the three partner companies refurbishing properties under the Pennine Investment Programme.

Apprentices acquire a range of practical skills and can focus on one particular trade in their third year. Calderdale College provides the off-site training element in one- or two-week blocks.

# ❑ 9.4 Graduate recruitment

The widening participation in higher education has led to increased numbers of graduates, with more diverse backgrounds, entering the job market. Graduates have much to commend them to employers. Most are intelligent, ambitious and enthusiastic, have fresh ideas, can solve problems, are unlikely to have developed bad working habits and are computer literate. These qualities should ensure they can make an early contribution to a specific job, as well as offering future management potential.

The 'downsides' include:

- Many will need initiation into the disciplines of the workplace
- Many will want a competitive salary and expect a high degree of responsibility early on
- Many will be looking for fully mapped-out training and career programmes
- Career indecisiveness/a propensity to leave after they have been trained
- Employers report a lack of inter-personal skills and a lack of business awareness.

---

**Good practice checklist: Graduate recruitment**

**Rationale**

✓ Be clear about the rationale for employing graduates and translate this into recruitment materials and selection criteria.

✓ Housing graduates from accredited CIH programmes will have completed a programme of learning which will equip them with the specialised knowledge and skills to operate effectively in a housing environment. However, unless a specific vocational qualification is needed, consider recruiting from a wide range of subject areas – any degree is a training in how to think.

✓ If commercial awareness is needed, look particularly at those with previous work experience, paid or unpaid.

**Selling the organisation/package**

✓ Talk to graduates in terms of their career, as opposed to their first job.

✓ As with all recruitment, sell the set of benefits which will make the position appealing. Research suggests graduates are most motivated by interesting and challenging work, followed by good colleagues, competitive salary and opportunities for skills development.

✓ Emphasis on issues such as homelessness, the environment, and social exclusion is likely to appeal to a supposedly more values-driven graduate market.

✓ Offer a competitive salary (benchmarking information is available from the Association of Graduate Recruiters (AGR)).

→

---

✓ Do not oversell the job – be clear about what is being offered and what exactly they will be doing.

✓ Consider whether positions can be reorganised and jobs expanded to include extra responsibilities which take advantage of graduate skills and abilities. (The number of graduate-level jobs has not grown to keep pace with the increased supply, resulting in many more graduates entering low level jobs.)

✓ Be realistic about the calibre of graduate you can expect to attract with your offer.

## Focus recruitment efforts

✓ Graduate Prospects reported in 2003, that 98% of students use the internet, with 80% using it every day.

✓ Research which universities might be most suitable to target eg specific disciplines. Do not ignore local universities. Develop relationships with relevant courses and tutors as a means of developing links with potential applicants. Linking up with universities which include employment placements as part of a housing course may be especially welcomed.

✓ Advertising on site at universities is usually very cheap or free – via websites, vacancy bulletins, notice boards.

✓ Less targeted advertising is available through the national graduate newspaper, Prospects Today or through national newspapers carrying regular graduate appointment features.

## Offer work experience

✓ Consider the range, from work experience in vacations to offering sandwich year placements.

✓ Contact university careers service for students who want experience eg advertise in work bulletins for 6-8 week placements.

## Careers fairs

✓ Plan ahead, places often have to be booked well in advance.

✓ Consider the appropriateness of different types of fairs.

✓ Make sure enough staff are on hand to answer queries.

✓ Take along recent graduates who can talk about their experience.

✓ Small organisations – many universities offer SME days (for small and medium sized enterprises/organisations), so they do not have to compete with the large graduate recruiters.

## Employer presentations

✓ Hold presentations or drop-in sessions on or off campus. Colleges will promote these amongst students.

## Recruitment rewards

✓ Consider 'golden hello' payments, paying off student loans or paying tuition fees/sponsorship as a means of attracting graduates.

■ **Graduate development schemes**

Research amongst graduates shows the importance they attach to training and development opportunities, together with the ability to study part-time. Many organisations have found the best way of providing these opportunities, and at the same time meeting their own need to develop their 'managers of the future', is through a structured graduate training scheme.

## Gee+ Graduate Training Scheme

The Gee+ graduate training programme was devised by a small group of London housing associations, to supply residential surveyors to the sector.

The surveyor programme is a full-time structured trainee work programme, leading to a RICS residential surveyors qualification. A building surveyor programme is also being developed. The participant has a two-year trainee employment contract with Gee+ and is paid a salary during the contract period. The employer chooses a trainee from the Gee+ pool of trainees (who have all gone through the Gee+ assessment centre) and pays HERA (the Gee+ business partner) for the placement of each trainee.

One of the core principles of Gee+ is the commitment to diversity in the selection process, with the aim to achieve 50% representation for women and BME candidates as well as attracting candidates with disabilities.

There is high demand for trainees who have completed the course. Housing management, IT and finance programmes are now in the pipeline. The scheme could also be developed in the future to enable employers to buy in to the programme for their existing staff.

## Southern Housing Group

Southern Housing Group introduced a Graduate Trainee Scheme in 2001 with the aim of recruiting high-quality graduates into a career in housing and regeneration. The Group is currently in their third year of running this scheme and to date have recruited seven graduate trainees.

The three year programme involves two years of general business acumen with one year's objective training in preparation for their first established position with the Group. During the first two years participants receive general training in all areas of the business, spending time in the main departments of the Group before moving into their specialist area in year 3.

Trainees are paid a competitive salary and are encouraged to meet realistic career goals by seeking professional training at the end of year 1. The Group also offers counselling and mentoring support (from a senior manager in the Group) once the trainee is in post.

## The Places for People Group

The Places for People Group sponsors placements on postgraduate housing degree courses at the London School of Economics (LSE). The placements are aimed at people from BME communities and the scheme was introduced in response to the under-representation of BME groups in housing. The scheme pays tuition fees and provides a bursary for living expenses. The Group reports success in recruiting excellent candidates, who have gone on to show strong loyalty to the organisation.

## HERA New Entrants into Housing Scheme

HERA has developed a scheme that identifies high potential trainees wanting to work in housing. Candidates attend an assessment centre which includes testing for general ability and verbal, numerical and IT skills, and a customer care interview. A pool of assessed candidates is available for employers to choose from.

## National Graduate Development Programme (NGDP)

The NGDP was set up in 2002 by the Employers' Organisation for Local Government in recognition of the need to recruit fresh talent and develop the managers of the future. Graduates undertake a rigorous assessment via interviews and an assessment centre. In addition a number of local authorities operate their own graduate training schemes.

---

### Good practice checklist: Graduate development schemes

✓ A thorough and timely induction to the workplace will be necessary, as the graduate may not have had previous employment experience. There is evidence that many graduates find starting work difficult, stressful and challenging.

✓ Consider the use of buddy systems and mentoring schemes (see Chapter 10). Mentoring has been found to be particularly useful as a means of: managing the transition to work; managing the new graduate's expectations; improving their confidence in career progression; and taking them beyond two year's service (a common point at which graduates seek alternative employment).

✓ Provide a career path that is financially rewarding eg increase salary at intervals subject to achieving agreed targets.

✓ Ensure the initial job offers early responsibility and freedom to act, in a supportive setting.

→

✓ Ensure a high quality training and development programme is in place that is tailored to the needs of their current work role and future career plans.

✓ Avoid very specific or narrow functions which may not take account of career indecision. Enable moves between functions to test alternative career directions.

✓ Appraise performance regularly and give feedback.

✓ In larger organisations, encourage networking amongst the graduate trainees in order to maintain momentum/motivation.

✓ Give consideration to other employees and resist obvious preferential treatment – minimise possible resentment by explaining the graduate's role to the rest of the team.

✓ Assess the value of the graduate to the organisation, both during and after the scheme. Have they added significant value before moving on? Retaining graduates is a key issue for employers to ensure the effort invested in the recruitment process does not go to waste.

✓ Manage carefully the period at the end of the scheme in order to avoid a training vacuum.

# CHAPTER 10

## INTEGRATION INTO THE ORGANISATION

This chapter considers the need to help new recruits integrate as quickly as possible into the organisation. It considers the main tools employers can use to ensure that the time invested in recruitment is not wasted by a high turnover rate in the first few months. It looks at:

- Effective induction
- The use of 'buddies'
- Mentoring systems

## ❏ 10.1 Why integration is so important

Having selected the best candidate for the job, the employer must ensure that the new recruit settles into the organisation quickly if they are to keep them in the long term. Research shows that this socialisation is as important as selection in determining the performance of newcomers and their attitudes towards their new job. Early and positive impressions made on new staff will remain with them for many months.

Without effective integration, new employees can get off to a bad start and never really understand the organisation or their role in it. This can lead to poor integration into the team, low morale, failure to work to their highest potential, absenteeism and, ultimately, resignation or dismissal. Effective integration will be particularly important for those recruits coming new to the sector from other backgrounds.

In the CIPD *Recruitment and Retention Survey* (2003), 27% of organisations reported retention difficulties at under six months' service. The costs of losing staff in the first few months of employment include: financial costs of recruiting and training a replacement, loss of productivity, lowering of morale for the remaining staff and possible damage to the organisation's reputation in the leaver's circle of contacts.

# ❑ 10.2 Induction

Induction is the process of familiarisation with the organisation and the new job. There is a large body of research showing the link between effective induction and the successful retention of employees in the first months of their employment.

## ■ Purpose of induction

The Industrial Society (now the Work Foundation) (1997) lists the five key objectives of induction, as ensuring new recruits:

- Settle into the new environment
- Develop the skills and knowledge they need to do their job
- Understand how their jobs relate to the rest of the organisation
- Understand the culture of the organisation and the standards of behaviour expected of them
- Become motivated and effective members of the workforce as quickly as possible.

A good induction programme will contain the following elements:

- Physical orientation – describing where the facilities are.
- Organisational orientation – showing how the employee fits into the team.
- Social orientation – introductions to colleagues and other staff.
- Health and safety information (statutory requirement).
- Explanation of employee's terms and conditions.
- Details of the organisation's history, products and services, culture, goals and values. This should include details of the organisation's approach to diversity.
- A clear outline of the job/role requirements, including the required level of performance and how the individual's performance feeds into the needs of the business.

(Adapted from CIPD *Quick Facts on Induction*)

## ■ Conventional induction 'events'

In many organisations, induction has traditionally been seen as a one-off event. This typically involves one or two days of formal training, usually involving presentations by senior managers about different aspects of the organisation.

This type of event can play a useful role, as one part of an induction process, and provided it is held soon after the employee starts:

- It can provide a useful opportunity for the new employee to meet with other new starters
- It can ensure that all new recruits are given a positive message and consistent information
- It is relatively straightforward to organise and can save managers' time by dealing with a group of new starters together.

However, this type of one-off event has several disadvantages, especially if it is used in isolation:

- It may take place several weeks or months after the new starter joins the organisation, which limits its usefulness
- If the group is too large it may be daunting and is unlikely to encourage participation
- The repetitious nature of the event for managers means it is likely to be fairly low down their list of priorities
- The content tends to be too generalised and of limited relevance to individual participants, who are likely to be cross-functional and of mixed ability
- The nature of the event means it is likely to contain too much information to be assimilated in a short time.

## ■ Induction as a process

In recent years, there has been an emphasis on achieving more effective induction in the housing sector. A key reason for this has been the widespread adoption of the Investors in People (IiP) standard. IiP demands that all training, including induction, is driven by the needs of the business, is relevant to the individual and is properly evaluated.

Increasingly then, induction is being seen as a process, which begins before the employee joins the organisation and leads into their continuous development. Induction is looked upon as the first stage in identifying training needs and it is important that managers are equipped to be able to work with the employee in recognising gaps in skills and knowledge. As part of the process, personal development plans (PDPs) may be drawn up, focusing on the development of the individual employee (see Chapter 11). It is never too early to demonstrate to employees that the organisation is prepared to invest in them in return for what they are contributing.

Typical key stages in the induction process are outlined in the following table.

| Stage | Task | Who is responsible |
|---|---|---|
| Recruitment | • Give information about job, location, conditions, etc | HR/recruiting manager |
| Pre-employment | • Keep in touch with those who have accepted an offer of employment<br>• Offer opportunity to meet future colleagues<br>• Send copies of documents relevant to new role<br>• Issue contract and terms and conditions<br>• Issue joining instructions | Line manager<br><br><br><br>HR |
| First day | • Introduce organisation, job requirements, initial tasks<br>• Meet immediate colleagues<br>• Explain induction programme/issue induction pack/checklist<br>• Completion of employee forms | Line manager<br><br>HR/Line Manager |
| First week | • Explain health and safety issues<br>• Tour of office<br>• Individual meetings with key colleagues<br>• Explain operation of probationary period, appraisal/performance system | HR/Safety Officer<br>Line manager |
| First month | • Corporate induction, if applicable<br>• Draw up personal development plan or training plan | Snr managers/HR<br>Line manager/<br>Training Officer |
| First 3 months | • Increased supervision/one-to-one meetings | Line manager |
| 3 months onwards | • Regular supervision/one-to-one meetings<br>• Review against personal development plan/continuous development | Line manager |
| 6 months | • Confirmation of end of probationary period, if applicable<br>• Review and evaluation of induction process | Line manager<br><br>Line manager/HR |

## Good practice checklist: Effective induction

**Planning induction programmes**

✓ Ensure responsibilities for induction are clearly defined. Induction of a specific employee should be the line manager's responsibility. HR should be responsible for overall induction policy, for developing programmes and courses, for implementing some aspects of induction and for evaluation of the induction process.

✓ Ensure 'inductors' are trained for the task.

✓ Vary the length and nature of the induction process to the nature of the job and the background of the new employee. A graduate with little work experience will have different needs from a senior manager. Ideally, all new employees should receive an individual induction programme reflecting their specific needs.

✓ Consider pursuing CIH accreditation of the programme, so enabling employees to gain the CIH Level 2 Certificate in Housing.

**Delivery of information**

✓ Deliver information in short bursts, over a period of time. Do not overload on first day.

✓ Concentrate on active learning tasks (eg encouraging employees to find out information for themselves by talking to colleagues).

✓ Ensure any written information or induction pack is well designed and contains accurate and up-to-date information.

✓ Consider use of computer based training packages or the intranet as flexible and cost effective methods of relaying certain information. For example, the Housing Projects Training Service produces a brief training CD, intended for staff new to housing associations. It includes 'lessons', followed by a quiz, on topics such as how associations are funded, regulated and governed and the current issues facing the housing sector.

✓ Issue written checklists to new recruits to enable them to monitor progress. Example checklists are available from several sources eg ACAS and CIPD.

✓ Be aware of the importance of socialisation issues (ie building relationships and also familiarisation with the organisation's values and culture).

✓ Ensure regular, frequent meetings with the line manager for three months after start date, providing an opportunity to ask questions and raise any concerns. Early resignations are far less likely to occur where people are able to voice difficulties.

**Employees who may need special attention**

✓ Ensure the induction programme includes all new staff (eg senior managers, part-time staff, temporary staff, and homeworkers).

✓ Consider the induction needs of existing employees who may be changing role, and those people returning after career breaks.

→

✓ Plan carefully to reduce any problems which may arise for employees with disabilities, (eg in terms of access, equipment or dealing with colleagues). Specialist advice is available from the Disability Employment Advisers of the Department for Work and Pensions.

✓ Ensure BME and other minority staff receive the same programme as other new starters but pay attention to any sensitivities (eg cultural or religious customs – see Chapter 13).

✓ Anticipate any potential difficulties either with the existing workforce or client group and prepare the ground for new employees. Examples of where additional support may be required would include a woman starting work in a male-dominated work area, or a BME appointment in a rural area with a small or non-existent BME community. The Diversity Team at the Employers' Organisation for Local Government produces *Diversity in the Districts* guidance.

### Evaluation

✓ Ensure the process is properly reviewed and evaluated. Methods include: analysing statistics on early leavers as a fairly crude measure of effectiveness; reviewing the process with new entrants (eg at the end of the probationary period); and asking questions about induction as part of the exit interview.

## Devon and Cornwall Housing Group

Devon and Cornwall HG has devised core training programmes for its key jobs. Each role has been broken down into core tasks, skills, relevant experience and competencies. The objectives of the programmes are:

- To form a basis for line managers and staff to identify competency in core activities
- To identify any training needs and to specify how these will be met
- To identify any performance issues.

The training programmes are intended to be used for all staff, but are especially useful for assessing new staff and enabling an induction training programme to be devised. The line manager completes a training programme analysis with the new starter in their first month. HR are responsible for arranging training courses. The line manager is responsible for arranging other training/development (eg on-the-job training, shadowing, attendance at meetings etc).

The core training programme forms part of each review meeting throughout the new starter's probationary period. HR confirm a new starter's employment at the end of the probationary period provided all criteria have been met.

# ❑ 10.3 Buddy systems

Increasingly, organisations are recognising the benefits of assigning an experienced worker to a new member of staff to support and assist them in settling into their job and the organisation. A buddy will usually be a peer colleague, working in a similar role and should not be a line manager or someone working in HR.

Buddies can provide, at very low cost to the organisation:
- Moral support
- Insights into the way the organisation works
- Answers to day-to-day queries
- Access to social networks
- Help with identifying and resolving early problems.

The key to the success of buddy systems is their informality. Informal information about the workplace is quickly and effectively disseminated (eg who is the best person to approach about a specific issue). A further advantage is the developmental experience it provides for the buddy.

························································································

### Aylesbury Vale District Council (AVDC)

As a supplement to their induction programme, AVDC provides each new starter with a key contact person within the team, who can help them find their way around the organisation, learn about key procedures and identify main contacts within and outside the council.

························································································

# ❑ 10.4 Mentoring

## ■ What is mentoring?

Mentoring is a popular concept that is used in a wide range of settings (eg for young people at risk or in helping homeless persons). In employment, mentoring is increasingly being used to support line management and professional development. It is a process by which managers can share the benefits of their knowledge and experience with other staff by giving guidance on personal development and career management.

The objective of mentoring is to help people improve their performance and reach their potential more quickly. It is about assisting people to establish solutions for themselves.

## ■ Mentoring to facilitate integration

Organisations use mentoring for a wide range of purposes (eg it is often used as a way of preparing established staff for new roles – see Chapter 11).

However, a key use is as part of induction:

- To help explain the formal and informal structure of the organisation
- To assist in the understanding of the culture – the norms, standards and values
- To enable personal and professional networks to be developed
- To help identify career opportunities, training and development needs, skills deficiencies and gaps in knowledge.

Mentoring is commonly used in graduate development programmes (see Chapter 9).

## ■ How does mentoring work?

New staff are matched with a committed and trained mentor. The mentor, who is a volunteer, will be an experienced person, in a more senior position, who ideally will have first-hand knowledge of the job the new recruit is doing. The mentor should not be the mentee's line manager – their role is to supplement and not replace the manager.

In a programme of regular and structured meetings, mentors provide advice, support and encouragement on how to handle problems and situations. In most schemes it is anticipated that there will be regular contact over a significant period of time, but that there will come a point when the mentoring relationship should end.

Career Opportunities for Ethnic Minorities (COFEM) has produced a mentoring training and process pack for use by the social housing sector. The pack contains full guidance on setting up a mentoring programme.

The Chartered Institute of Housing promotes mentoring as an important part of its professional development programme APEX, and is piloting a generic mentoring scheme which all CIH members will be able to access at any stage of their career.

## ■ Advantages for the organisation

A mentoring scheme can:

- Improve self-confidence, increase motivation, widen horizons and raise performance for the new staff member
- Expand the skills and understanding of managers
- Contribute to achieving a more proportional representation of certain under-represented staff (eg women, people with disabilities, BME staff) in management positions
- Provide a way of recognising and developing future high achievers
- Be a cost effective form of management development
- Provide insights into problems in the organisation
- Improve communication through the promotion of discussion and understanding.

---

### Good practice checklist: Mentoring

✓ Mentoring can be a very effective tool, but only as a complement to other strategies of development or support.

✓ Mentors need a range of qualities, including good listening skills, self-confidence and the ability to relate, be supportive, be non-judgmental and to give clear and honest feedback.

✓ The matching process is crucial – there must be a strong base of trust between the mentor and mentee. Mentees should be able to change their mentor if they choose.

✓ Clear objectives and expectations are important from the outset, to enable effective relationships to develop and to enable success to be evaluated.

✓ Arrangements, including confidentiality rules, should be formalised in a mentoring contract.

✓ Meetings should be set in advance and have an agreed agenda. Outcomes should be recorded and progress reviewed.

---

## Bradford Community Housing Trust (BCHT)

BCHT operates an Area Coach service, providing support for both new and existing employees. Area Coaches have an identified job role within the organisation covering practical, task-related coaching. Coaches have assisted BCHT to introduce:

- Robust induction
- 'User friendly' systems and 'which button to push' guides
- Individual support for staff returning after absence
- New policies and procedures

They also assist BCHT by championing and promoting good practice.

Coaches operate by working closely with managers to ensure that employees receive the appropriate support and training to enable them to deliver the best quality services. By working locally they ensure that the ongoing system/process support needs of staff are addressed.

The Coaches are flexible and offer support using a variety of methods ranging from a telephone coaching session lasting a few minutes to a detailed 1-1 programme covering all office processes and IT systems which may last several weeks. BCHT regards this flexibility as the key to the success of the service.

# CHAPTER 11

## PERSONAL DEVELOPMENT AND CAREER STRUCTURE

This chapter considers how providing opportunities for staff to develop their skills and further their careers can improve motivation and encourage loyalty. It looks at:

- Opportunities for internal promotion and succession planning
- Other development opportunities, such as lateral promotion, job enrichment, secondments and work shadowing
- Training and qualifications
- Evolving practice in career management and the use of personal development plans

## ❏ 11.1 Introduction

There is a vast body of research showing the link between employee development and retention. In a major study for the CIPD in 2003, Purcell et al showed that positive perceptions of career opportunities are among the most powerful determinants of employee commitment to an organisation.

MORI research in the housing sector in 2002 showed that training and development was high on the general public's list of factors when choosing a job. It was the benefit most frequently mentioned by employers (after pay) in recruitment literature and yet career progression was the main explanation given by HR directors as to why people leave housing associations and this was corroborated by the leavers themselves.

In 2003, MORI found fairly low satisfaction amongst existing staff in the sector regarding opportunities for personal development. The ratings for line management also underlined the need to focus on improving career management of their staff.

Successfully improving retention through development is a long-term strategy and means examining the whole approach to employee development from the recruitment process all the way through their time with the organisation. The aim at all times is to make the employee feel valued by demonstrating concern for their future career as well as their current contribution.

## ❑ 11.2 Opportunities for promotion

Many staff (often the better performers) are career-minded and will not stay long in an organisation that denies them the opportunity to advance upwards. Organisations need to demonstrate to staff that they can progress within the organisation through an open and fair advancement policy.

### ■ Recruiting internally where practicable

Organisations need to achieve a recruitment balance between bringing in fresh blood from outside and satisfying the aspirations of existing staff. Promotion of staff within an organisation can be a positive reflection of an effective recruitment system. It is encouraging and motivating to see a promotion system working fairly.

There is an assumption within the housing sector that it is a requirement of equalities legislation/good practice to advertise all posts externally. This is not the case, provided the organisation can demonstrate clear policies on recruitment and staff development and a clearly stated aim of looking to balance both.

There are, however, a number of circumstances where external recruitment is likely to be appropriate:
- The necessary skills and knowledge do not exist and would require a substantial investment in training to achieve.
- Where there is a desire to change culture and values, it may only be possible to do this by bringing in people externally.
- If the workforce is predominantly one sex or ethnic group, recruiting externally will be necessary to attempt to improve diversity. A policy of recruiting internally in these circumstances may amount to unlawful indirect discrimination.
- Senior appointments, for reasons of probity.

Appointment from within must always be carefully managed. Organisations should have transparent and consistent procedures to avoid suspicions of favouritism. Candidates should be shortlisted against pre-determined role requirements and assessed in the same way as when recruiting external staff. Appointment should always be based on merit.

It is important that internal vacancies are advertised in such a way that all employees will see them (including, for example, staff working at home). A policy of internal promotion should be kept under review and its impact assessed over time (eg in terms of impact on particular groups of staff).

...........................................................................

## Circle 33 Housing Group

It is Circle 33's policy to advertise all posts internally, before recruiting externally, unless there is good reason not to.

They have found this policy to be successful in terms of:
- Retaining valuable staff, by providing opportunities for them to progress
- Motivating existing staff, by sending the message that there are opportunities for advancement within the organisation
- Achieving greater representation of BME staff in higher level posts
- Increased speed and reduced costs for recruitment and integration of new staff.

Of 700 staff, 149 have been promoted or seconded or are acting up into more senior roles.

...........................................................................

## ■ Succession planning

Succession planning involves identifying individuals with the attributes to be promoted and providing them with appropriate experience when the opportunity arises (eg through assignments, management experience or role expansion).

In the past, the emphasis in succession planning was on filling jobs. More recently, and as a response to problems of high turnover in many sectors, the emphasis has moved to implementing strategies to develop and retain individuals.

...........................................................................

## Bromford Housing Group

Bromford HG has reversed its ratio of internal/external recruitment, so that 75% of team leaders and above are now recruited internally. This has enabled the Group to shift the balance of expenditure from recruitment to staff development.

The Group carries out succession planning interviews for managerial posts. The main considerations include: Are possible successors in place? What are their career aspirations? Do these reflect organisational needs? Can they be met? What developmental experiences can be given?

Through targeted training, development and coaching, the Group aims to pre-empt staff thinking about leaving the organisation.

...........................................................................

## Portsmouth City Housing Service

The Housing Service has developed a programme of 'ethical succession', for staff aspiring to management positions. Entry to the programme is via a transparent application process. Once accepted, delegates benefit from a 15-month development opportunity which comprises:

- Formal courses linked to management theory and good practice
- Opportunities for expansion through involvement with in-house projects/working parties
- Support of a mentor

Progress is assessed against the agreed competency framework for all managers. The programme is due to be rolled out to all levels of staff.

## ■ Restructuring to increase promotion opportunities

Though contrary to the overall trend for flatter structures, organisations may find it possible to provide a structure which allows greater opportunity for staff to progress.

## Derby Homes

Derby Homes has developed a grading structure for Maintenance Surveyors, enabling them to progress through the grade based on a combination of experience, qualifications and personal development. A grading assessment panel sits quarterly to consider applications for progression, submitted by employees with the support of their manager.

The new structure was introduced in response to:

- Difficulties in recruiting and retaining surveyors, a post which was critical to the organisation's investment and regeneration programme
- Frustration with the existing scheme of annual incremental progression, allowing no flexibility to reward skills and achievement
- The desire to instil a culture of continual professional development, in order to develop the organisation's skills base and encourage employee responsibility for their own development.

Managers wanted the flexibility of having a single grade and a broad job description which would enable them to establish teams with a balance of experience and skills.

→

The scheme includes four trainee posts, who are recruited below the entry grade, and are offered a training programme to enable them to access the full grade. The advertising strategy for these posts has included leaflet distribution within the BME communities in Derby, in an attempt to increase the diversity of the workforce in this area.

## ❏ 11.3 Other development opportunities

The efficiency drive within many organisations, leading to flatter structures, has meant a reduction in opportunities for promotion.

In these circumstances, it is important to be able to offer employees the chance to continue to grow and feel valued, without having to change employer. Some options include:

- Sideways promotion
- Job enrichment
- Internal and external secondments
- Shadowing
- Broader development opportunities

Whilst it may not be possible for smaller associations to offer some of the more sophisticated or formal employee development activities, it is likely that organisations can find informal ways of providing opportunities and encouraging skills development. Alternatively, smaller organisations may choose to collaborate in order to help build a career path for their staff.

### Horizon Housing Group

In response to staff concerns over career opportunities within the Group and in order to retain talented staff, Horizon HG has introduced a career development framework. The framework includes:

- Management development training/qualifications training
- Work shadowing/coaching
- Mentoring (joint scheme with Hyde HG, West Kent HA, Hexagon HA – see below)
- Internal and external secondment
- Acting up (taking on the full responsibilities of a more senior role on a short term basis)
- Additional duties (undertaking duties in addition to the substantive post on a short-term basis)
- PATH and COFEM schemes (career development schemes for BME staff).

## Sanctuary Housing Association

Sanctuary HA has a career progression policy which aims to:
- Fully utilise the potential and existing skills of all staff
- Equip staff with the experience and skills that will enable them to develop their careers
- Enable the association to attract and retain high performing staff

The association operates a number of different schemes:
- Pathways – staff who are interested in pursing a career in a new field of work are given the opportunity to gain an insight into that area and assistance to develop the required skills. Staff may be involved in work shadowing, mentoring and attending relevant training courses. Regular progress meetings will also be held.
- Graduate Trainee Scheme – a tailored programme of work experience and training.
- NVQs – the association is a registered centre for NVQs in Housing and Social Care.
- Management Development – managers can study for the Certificate in Management which leads to membership of the Chartered Management Institute.

### ■ Sideways 'promotion'

Lateral moves to other departments enable employees to move into different areas that are suited to their capabilities and interests. This can open up the possibility of a different career path, especially where the area is one which is expanding. For example, the growth in importance of community development in some organisations, has provided a lateral move for housing management staff.

### ■ Job enrichment/stretch projects

Job enrichment focuses on making a role more satisfying and motivating for staff, for example, by increasing variety, responsibility or autonomy. Organisations can consider:
- Reviewing responsibilities between individuals in a team in order to achieve a better alignment between organisational requirements and employees' developmental objectives
- Temporarily enriching jobs by giving employees interesting assignments or project work
- Empowering/giving greater autonomy by allowing employees more independence, discretion and self-direction
- Automating some of the more routine elements of a job

## Northern Counties Housing Association

High turnover of administrative staff within housing services led NCHA to
redesign and re-evaluate the role. The new post of Customer Services Officer
was established, with particular emphasis on the role being the first point of
enquiry for tenants. An important part of the exercise was to give the post
higher status and value within the organisation. Existing staff transferred to
the higher grade job, with a development programme in place. Job
satisfaction was seen to increase markedly and turnover reduced to zero as a
result of the changes.

## ■ Secondments

Secondment involves the temporary transfer of an employee to another department
or to another organisation.

### Advantages

- Offers the chance of developing knowledge and skills, with the benefit of
  continuity of employment
- Useful for resourcing short-term projects
- Improved communications between departments/organisations.

### Disadvantages

- There may be difficulties in filling the secondee's substantive post on a
  temporary basis, leading to a possible disruption to service
- Possible reluctance on the part of the secondee to return to their original post.

---

### Good practice checklist: Secondments

✓ Does the organisation have a written secondment procedure that is well
publicised to staff?

✓ Is it possible to identify posts suitable for secondment?

✓ Are secondment positions advertised to the widest possible audience?

✓ Is an effective induction provided for inward secondees?

✓ Are secondments carefully monitored throughout the placement?

✓ Is there a review of how knowledge and experiences gained by the secondee
have benefited both them and the organisation?

✓ In the case of external secondments, is there absolute clarity between the two
organisations at the outset over responsibilities and obligations (eg for
performance management, disciplinary matters etc).

## London Borough of Brent

The post of Corporate Support Officer in the Chief Executive's Office is reserved to provide an annual internal secondment opportunity for a member of staff. The post is advertised across the authority in the Brent Job Bulletin and postholders have come from a variety of disciplines. The post has a wide remit and provides the employee with a unique development opportunity, working at the hub of the authority.

## The Ridings Housing Association

In 2001/2 the Association's avoidable leavers turnover was 26%. The majority of people were leaving for reasons of career development/lack of opportunity within the organisation, and this was also highlighted as an issue by staff in the employee survey. As a relatively small organisation (63 employees), with a flattish structure, the association was finding it difficult to provide developmental opportunities for staff. In addition, the recruitment policy was restrictive with regard to internal recruitment.

The association piloted the use of secondments as learning opportunities for real vacancies, and as a result two employees were promoted into permanent posts. The policy was redrafted to remove the requirement to advertise externally for all posts. All vacancies are now immediately advertised to existing employees as opportunities to act up or for secondment.

The Ridings reports the benefits have been:
- Reduced turnover (19% in 2002/3), together with cost savings on recruitment
- Improved morale
- Improved customer service
- Internal promotions have resulted in an opportunity to appoint new front-line staff, positively recruited from the local community, so enhancing diversity of the workforce.

## Race Equality Network

The Race Equality Network was set up to improve performance on race equality issues in the housing sector. The network offers housing employees the opportunity to undertake short-term voluntary secondments to build on their knowledge of diversity issues.

## ■ Work-shadowing

Work-shadowing is a process whereby an individual follows someone in their work role for a period of time. Through observing, experiencing and listening, they gain a deeper knowledge and understanding of the person's role. As well as gaining broader experience, the shadower may also identify an alternative career path.

## ■ Mentoring

Mentoring is discussed in detail in Chapter 10. Mentoring can be a particularly effective way of supporting women and other minority group employees' progression in an organisation because of the role models and network of support it provides.

### Horizon HG, Hyde HG, West Kent HA and Hexagon HA

These organisations are working in partnership to provide a mentoring scheme for their staff. The goals of the partnership include:

- Creating career development and personal growth opportunities
- Providing opportunities for staff to share skills, experience and good practice
- Creating connections throughout the partner associations
- Enhancing the work environment
- Increasing staff retention and job satisfaction.

Training for the mentors and mentees is provided by the partner associations on a cost-sharing basis. The HR departments of the associations are responsible for monitoring the scheme and its outputs, and reporting annually to the four senior management teams.

## ■ Broader development opportunities

Offering opportunities for individuals to develop their skills and careers outside the confines of their current role is a further way of ensuring they feel valued.

### Space New Living Ltd

With the intention of enriching employee's lives, a popular benefit at Space has been the introduction of a personal development budget for each member of staff towards fulfilling something they want to do. Space does not insist that the money is spent on anything work-related, and examples have included flying lessons and a cookery course.

## ❏ 11.4 Training and qualifications

Whilst the main objective of training is to enhance staff performance, its role in improving employee commitment should not be underestimated. Specifically:

- Recognised training and qualifications are valued by staff and help to retain (and attract) employees

- Training improves skills and knowledge and helps ensure that staff feel confident and competent to carry out their role. This is particularly important for staff new to the housing sector, who will need assistance in developing their subject knowledge quickly.

- Training can provide opportunities to broaden experience beyond the employee's current job role.

### ■ Recent developments in training

There has been a considerable shift in recent years in approaches to training within organisations.

- The emphasis has moved from *training* to *learning*, with individuals taking greater ownership of their own learning needs. This trend is based on the premise that people learn more when they have control over what is learned and how it is achieved.

- There is movement away from training as a separate formal activity and towards learning as a mainstream part of the job. In particular, the technique of coaching has emerged as an informal approach to on-the-job development. Coaching supports the development of new skills, based on a close relationship between the individual and usually their line manager, who is experienced in the task/role. The manager as coach helps individuals to develop by giving them the opportunity to perform an increasing range of tasks, and by helping them to learn from their experiences.

- New ways of delivering learning have developed, largely as a response to increasingly flexible working practices eg distance and open learning, e-learning and 'bite-sized' learning.

---

**Good practice checklist: Training**

Changes to training needs and provision in the housing sector were mentioned in Chapter 2. There is much that individual organisations can do to ensure they are able to address current skills shortages and to meet the training needs of an increasingly diverse workforce, from a range of backgrounds. (Note: the role of structured trainee schemes is discussed in Chapter 9. Leadership and management training is discussed in Chapter 3).

→

---

**Keep training relevant**

✓ Ensure training is planned and linked to organisational needs, rather than arranged on an ad hoc basis. Many organisations in the sector are addressing this as a result of seeking IiP accreditation, which encourages looking at training and development processes in a more detailed and structured way.

✓ Recognise the role of the line manager in working with staff to recognise skills and knowledge gaps and in supporting the development of a learning environment.

✓ Consider in-house training programmes as a means of meeting particular needs. Seeking accreditation for in-house courses is an important way of integrating training into the workplace environment (see box opposite).

✓ Establish dialogue with colleges to ensure external courses reflect the dynamic and diverse nature of the sector.

**Encouraging all employees**

✓ Be flexible in terms of the type and range of vocational and qualifications training the organisation will support.

✓ Keep pace with new and flexible ways of delivering training (eg encourage distance learning where unable to release staff and/or to enable staff to study to suit their own lifestyle and commitments).

✓ Ensure that training opportunities are provided in a fair and equitable way by monitoring take-up. In particular, part-time workers and older workers can sometimes be overlooked.

✓ Be innovative in ways of encouraging employees to study externally (eg through sponsorships or bursaries).

✓ Recognise training achievements.

**Use training to broaden experience**

✓ Train to build new skills, rather than merely reinforcing old ones.

**Evaluation**

✓ Evaluate training in the longer term, in order to try and evaluate the learning (rather than the course itself). Take account of the wider contribution training can make, eg in terms of improving motivation and increasing loyalty.

## CIH flexible accreditation

The CIH has developed new ways of working with housing providers to provide a structured framework for staff training, which will also enable employees to achieve a nationally recognised qualification. This flexible new approach enables the CIH to match qualifications, or individual units within qualifications, with the training and development requirements of employers.

- The YMCA in England approached the CIH to discuss a development programme for staff to prepare them for the challenge of Supporting People. In 2002 the CIH accredited the YMCA Learning Zone to deliver the Level 2 Certificate in Housing and the Level 3 National Certificate in Housing directly. Staff follow a programme of learning which develops their skills and also leads to a CIH qualification. The YMCA reports significant improvements in motivation, self-confidence and performance in staff that have taken part in the programmes.

- In 2000 Portsmouth City Housing Service carried out a review of its recruitment, training and development functions. The Council decided to seek direct accreditation from the CIH to deliver the Level 3 National Certificate in Housing to staff. Staff study for a qualification which develops their skills in the areas of benefits advice and housing management and maintenance.

## West Lothian Council

West Lothian Council won the *Outstanding Achievement in Social Housing (Scotland)* Award in 2003 for its Employee Development Strategy.

Five years previously, the Housing Services workforce was mostly unqualified. Training was ad hoc, untargeted and there was no follow-up or evidence of changing practice as a result. As the service requirements changed, the council recognised that in order to meet new demands and expectations, training needed to become part of the culture within Housing Services. In short, they wanted to be a 'thinking and learning organisation'.

The Housing Department, in partnership with West Lothian College, devised a unique system of joint planning, teaching and assessment for courses, leading to staff gaining housing qualifications. Housing Services managers deliver the learning events and assess assignments alongside West Lothian College staff. CIH has accredited the college to award a Level 2 Certificate in Housing and a Level 4 Diploma course, enabling a wide range of staff to gain a nationally recognised qualification.

→

A complete programme of events has been drawn up to meet different needs:

- A foundation course for all staff which consists of one full day per week for five months.
- The Level 4 CIH Diploma course is offered on a day release basis for two years.
- Shorter courses are available for specific skills development eg Buildings Awareness or Mediation.
- A Management Development Course (leading to an Institute of Management Certificate Level 3) for those wishing to move into management.
- A leisure programme of 'stress busters'.

A career development scheme is in place using competencies based on national occupational standards for housing. The scheme leads to monetary reward for staff. New staff take part in a comprehensive induction programme which identifies their existing strengths and knowledge so that future training is tailor-made to their particular requirements. A personal development plan for all members of staff includes a detailed training programme, with continual assessment and review.

Since 2000 the number of staff with a recognised housing qualification has increased from 16 to 113. In addition, the Council reports that participating staff show increased motivation, and that the strategy has led to a stronger focus on promotion and advancement.

## ❏ 11.5 Career management

Traditionally, active career management has tended to concentrate on people of particular value to the organisation (typically senior managers and their potential successors). For the majority of staff, a brief discussion during their annual performance appraisal is likely to be their only experience of career management.

However, skill shortages and continuing problems in attracting staff highlight the importance of developing the capability of all employees to the full. Organisations are beginning to widen their career management activities to embrace the whole workforce.

The challenge for organisations is to build and retain the talent they need now and in the future, while satisfying employee career aspirations. In recognition of the tensions inherent in this, the most effective model of career management is likely to be a dual strategy of targeted career management for key posts, together with more universal support for the majority of staff.

## ■ Career management activities

Career management processes can include:

- Development-focused appraisals which include career aspirations and options for career development. It is important that such discussions are held separately from discussions about performance.
- Internal career coaches (providing group workshops on career management and one-to-one advice).
- Provision of web-based information and guidance on career management and on opportunities in the organisation.
- Training for all employees on how to manage their own careers.
- Informal career support (eg advice provided by HR).
- Networks aimed at particular groups of employees (eg women's networks or support groups for disabled employees to encourage progression and development).

............................................................

## COFEM

The Career Opportunities for Ethnic Minorities (COFEM) initiative aims to improve the opportunities for BME employees in housing. The initiative works through groups of housing employers coming together to provide programmes for selected BME employees aimed at increasing their personal and career development. The programme includes mentoring, secondments, shadowing, visits, seminars and information exchanges.

............................................................
............................................................

## Federation of Black Housing Organisations (FBHO)

FBHO has launched a national staff network – NETWORK + which aims to ensure that the sector continues to value and mainstream race and diversity issues. It will also help facilitate discussion around BME staff involvement in all parts of the social housing sector.

NETWORK+ is open to all staff working in housing and will:

- Create a platform through which FBHO can support staff during their employment in the sector
- Assist individuals in their growth and development as emerging leaders
- Support members to make the most of their talents and potential
- Act as a catalyst for change

A key objective is to assist in addressing issues of under-representation of BME staff and board members and in delivering excellent and appropriate services in partnership with BME communities.

............................................................

---

### Good practice checklist: Supporting career management

✓ A career management strategy is unlikely to be effective unless it is driven and promoted by senior managers who fully accept the business case for it.

✓ A robust performance management system must be in place, involving regular two-way dialogue between the employee and line manager.

✓ The role of line managers is essential. To take the lead in supporting the career development of their staff, line managers will need thorough training (eg in basic techniques for recognising talent or in skills such as coaching) as well as proactive support from HR.

✓ Line managers must be encouraged to give sufficient priority to the career management of their teams (eg reward managers who are good at developing staff).

✓ Employees need appropriate support and guidance to enable them to set up their own career development activities. Self-managed development can be encouraged by the use of Personal Development Plans (see below).

✓ Employers must be alert to career progression barriers faced by certain employee groups (eg older workers, women, ethnic minorities, part-time workers, returning employees). They should monitor and evaluate staff promotion and take-up of career development opportunities by ethnicity, gender, etc.

✓ Consider positive development schemes for those who are disadvantaged. Ensure support mechanisms are in place outside of the line management structure.

✓ Organisations should seek feedback from employees (eg in staff surveys) on which specific aspects of career management are working/not working.

---

## ■ Personal Development Plans

Personal Development Plans are short documents mapping out how a person can develop skills and progress in their job. They are hugely beneficial in demonstrating organisational commitment to the achievement of personal development goals and longer-term career aims. Ideally, every employee should have a PDP.

### Benefits/features

- PDPs usually require individuals to take personal ownership of their learning and development.
- They are unique to the individual, who is responsible, with their manager, for drawing them up and for progress in achieving aims.
- They are useful for managing the development of a new employee (see Chapter 10).

- They offer a way to map out a clear career path within the organisation, by allowing individuals to identify where they want to go and how best this can be achieved. Longer term objectives are usually broken down into short term goals.
- Regular review and updating of the PDP is essential, usually as part of a development-focused appraisal. Review periods will depend upon timescales in the PDP.

# CHAPTER 12

# PAY, REWARD AND RECOGNITION

This chapter summarises the research evidence on the link between pay and staff turnover and explores a number of pay, reward and recognition strategies which have the potential to improve retention. It looks at the importance of:

- Ensuring that payment systems are perceived by staff to operate fairly (objective systems that reward contribution)
- Focusing activities on those groups that are most likely to leave for higher pay
- Making the total pay and benefits package hard for competitors to replicate (flexible benefits and total reward)
- Recognition

## ❏ 12.1 Link between pay and turnover

It is widely believed that there is a clear and significant link between pay and staff turnover. A large body of research shows that, in practice, the situation is more complicated. Whilst some of the research appears to be inconclusive and even contradictory, it seems possible to draw the following conclusions:

- Most people are unlikely to leave a job in which they are broadly happy in order to secure more pay. They only think about leaving when they are dissatisfied about some other aspect of the job.
- Employees who are dissatisfied and thinking of leaving will only be deterred from doing so in the short term if they are given a pay rise.
- Whilst pay rarely motivates positively, perceptions of unfairness in payment arrangements do emerge as a demotivator. This is most likely to relate to perceptions of unfairness about the distribution of rewards within the organisation (as opposed to what other employers are paying).
- Certain groups of employees, for a variety of reasons, tend to be more money-orientated and are more likely to resign to secure higher pay than others. This category includes the lowest paid of all, people who are genuinely underpaid compared to their peers, and high-flyers (or the headhunted class).
- The reward package must meet the basic needs of employees. In some areas, notably London and South East England, the higher cost of living means a higher salary is needed.

The research evidence and experience of organisations suggests that throwing money at the problem of staff turnover will do no more than provide a temporary solution. However, there are measures organisations can consider in using pay policy to improve retention. The reconfiguration of pay and reward schemes can be important, as can be the development of a valued benefits package.

## ❏ 12.2 Ensuring fairness

Perception of unfairness in payment arrangements is a greater cause of employee turnover than the simple desire to earn more money. Organisations wishing to improve staff retention must adopt pay systems that are objective, and are seen by staff to be objective. This will usually require:

- Some kind of job evaluation scheme where roles are graded according to an objective assessment of their worth (and which may involve comparison with market rates)
- An element which recognises the contribution employees make to the organisation.

### ■ Rewarding contribution

The most common methods of pay that reward contribution are:

- Individual performance related pay (IPRP) – pay levels or bonus earnings are based on appraisal of an employee's performance against previously set objectives, usually as part of a performance management system.
- Competency based pay – schemes measure what the individual is bringing to the job, unlike traditional IPRP schemes, which measure outputs. A direct link is created between the acquisition, improvement and effective use of skills and competencies and the individual's pay.
- Contribution pay – combines elements of performance and competency based pay schemes by recognising the results that employees have produced and the competencies that have been used to achieve them. Unlike performance pay, contribution pay does not solely provide a direct incentive for achieving a designed set of targets. Instead, and in common with a competency-based system, it also emphasises the developmental progress required of employees.
- Team-based pay – links employee's earnings to how well or badly a department or section performs. The aim of team-based pay is to strengthen the team through incentives, building a coherent, mutually supportive group of people with a high level of involvement.
- Organisation-based pay – schemes are based on larger groups than teams, for example, divisions or the whole organisation.

(Definitions drawn from Employers Organisation website: Pay and Rewards section)

The main features of each approach are summarised in the following table.

| Scheme | Advantages/benefits | Disadvantages/difficulties |
|---|---|---|
| Individual Performance Related Pay (IPRP) | • Improved employee, and organisational, performance<br>• Links reward to individual performance and recognises effort and improvement<br>• Links reward to key business objectives | • Focus on individual goals can undermine team work, especially where targets are task driven<br>• Focus on short-term objectives, rather than a longer-term strategy<br>• Can detrimentally affect appraisal process due to focus on financial reward for achieving targets rather than developmental needs |
| Competency-based pay | • Increased skills and flexibility in the workplace<br>• Rewards non-task related behaviours, such as supporting colleagues<br>• Effective way for organisations to convey what they expect from employees<br>• Service objectives (eg customer focus) can be closely associated with remuneration | • No measure of productivity<br>• Little judgement on how effective the acquisition of competencies is to organisational performance<br>• Judgements about people's behaviour may be less than objective<br>• Increased demand for training and increased training costs<br>• Employers may pay for skills/competencies rarely used |
| Contribution pay | • More rounded view of employee performance<br>• Motivates employees to achieve higher levels of performance and skill<br>• Likely to be viewed by employees as a fairer system, as it rewards both skill and contribution<br>• Good way of communicating strategic vision, through the definition of expected performance and competence | • Relatively new concept and there is limited evidence of its effectiveness to date<br>• Potentially complex as managers have to assess both outputs and inputs |
| Team-based pay | • Positively encourages team working and co-operation<br>• Effective way of cascading objectives defined by senior management and of clarifying priorities within a team<br>• Can assist in bringing change in cultural attitude, particularly with the introduction of customer-focused working practices<br>• Peer group pressure can help raise performance of the whole team | • Can be difficult to identify targets that genuinely reflect group effort<br>• Does not usually differentiate between high and low performers, which can cause resentment<br>• Can take time for teams to work together effectively. Team-building training may be necessary<br>• May adversely affect relationships between teams |
| Organisation-based pay | • Encourages wider co-operation across the organisation<br>• Increases awareness of contribution to the total effort of the organisation<br>• Provides a more obvious link with the organisation and its ability to pay<br>• May encourage greater flexibility in ways of working to increase productivity | • Direct incentive value tends to be weak as link between daily work and bonus might seem remote |

(Adapted from Employers Organisation website: Pay and Rewards section)

. . . . . . . . . . . . . . . . . . . . . . . . . . . . . . . . . . . . . . . . . . . . . . . . . . . . . . . . . . . . . . . . . . .

## The Peabody Trust

The Peabody Trust's contribution pay scheme, introduced in 2001, enables progression linked to the achievement of individual objectives and demonstration of core competencies. The Trust has found the scheme to be robust and effective:

- In 2003, 100% of employee assessments were returned by managers within the given deadline
- Only six appeals were received, from a total of 511 staff
- Monitoring shows internal consistency between assessments and a reasonably normal distribution in terms of average, good and exceptional performance.

Further, whilst it is difficult to identify a clear causal link, the scheme is believed to have been effective in reducing staff turnover.

The Trust consider the success of the scheme is due to:

- A high level of staff understanding – achieved by communicating the scheme widely through various channels
- Close attention to the training/education of managers
- A well-established, coherent system of 1-1s between employees and their line managers.

. . . . . . . . . . . . . . . . . . . . . . . . . . . . . . . . . . . . . . . . . . . . . . . . . . . . . . . . . . . . . . . . . . .

---

### Good practice checklist: Relating pay to contribution

**Planning the scheme**

✓ Be clear about the objectives of the scheme. Is the scheme the right one to deliver those objectives?

✓ Ensure the scheme reflects the organisational culture.

✓ Be clear what the scheme is rewarding – must be able to identify what needs to be measured on a fair and accurate basis.

✓ Ensure that the scheme is based on the foundation of a sound payment system. The scheme will not be an effective substitute for adequate base rates of pay.

✓ Is there an effective performance management system in place? How will the scheme fit with this?

✓ Keep it simple – if too complex to administer or difficult for employees to understand it is likely to fail.

✓ Consider how the scheme will apply to certain groups of staff (eg new starters and trainees, temporary employees, part-time employees, staff on maternity leave).

✓ What resources are available (eg for consultation, communication and training).

✓ Consider the best time to introduce the scheme. Is the timescale realistic? Consider piloting the scheme before full roll-out.

→

---

### Achieving staff buy-in

✓ Involve line managers and a range of employees in developing the scheme. Ensure trade union or other representatives are involved from the outset.

✓ Ensure the scheme is transparent and objective.

✓ Communicate clearly details of the scheme prior to introducing it.

✓ Manage expectations carefully.

### Operation

✓ Ensure line managers are equipped to manage the scheme in question (eg to define performance objectives properly, to assess performance fairly or to assess competencies).

✓ Be clear about what is expected from employees in terms of their contribution and ensure that rewards properly reflect contribution.

✓ Ensure employees play an active role in reviewing their own performance and development needs and are involved in setting future objectives.

### Payment

✓ Consider how and when payment will be made. Consider one-off, non-consolidated bonuses rather than consolidating increases into basic pay. In this way employees have to keep meeting targets or competencies.

✓ In the case of discretionary payment schemes, ensure that arrangements comply with regulatory restrictions, eg Schedule 1 of the Housing Act 1996.

✓ Consider whether the bonus is big enough to be an incentive for staff.

✓ Ensure there are sufficient resources for contribution payments to be attained by most employees (it is unlikely that any motivational effect can be achieved if only a small percentage of employees can receive it).

✓ Is there sufficient differentiation between average and outstanding contribution?

### Appeals, monitoring and review

✓ What appeals procedure will there be?

✓ Build in consistency checks to ensure assessment of contribution is fair (ie across departments and employee groups eg women, BME staff, part-time workers).

✓ Evaluate the scheme annually with a more fundamental review every three to five years.

# ■ Rewarding length of service

A further approach is to reward people for remaining with an organisation. The evidence is unclear as to whether such schemes have any impact on increasing staff retention. Examples of initiatives include:

### Short-term incentives

- Retention bonuses that pay out after a set period of time.
- Cash-based profit sharing.

### Long-term incentives

- Incremental pay increases after each year of service.
- Long service awards.
- Share option schemes.
- Final salary pensions.
- Entitlement to benefits after x years service. Examples include entitlement to additional holiday or to a sabbatical, whereby an employee can take time off work, paid or unpaid, over and above usual holiday entitlement. Under a paid sabbatical scheme, an organisation may expect the employee to use the time to develop a skill that will help improve performance on return to work.

........................................................................................

## Circle 33 Housing Trust

Circle 33 has introduced unpaid sabbaticals of up to one year, for qualifying staff with three years continuous service. This is a retention measure, in response to information from exit interviews and staff surveys. The Trust reports that the policy is viewed very favourably by staff, even though it is likely relatively few will take it up.

........................................................................................

# ❏ 12.3 Focusing on the market where it matters

As the research findings outlined above suggest, there are specific groups of staff for whom it may well be necessary to target salary increases.

# ■ High-flyers

The retention of these employees is particularly desirable because, as individuals, they have the capacity to make a real difference to the success of an organisation. These staff are likely to require individually negotiated packages which take account of their market worth.

## ■ Uncompetitive pay

In cases where pay rates for specific groups of staff are uncompetitive and turnover is high, there is a need to provide clear evidence about comparative pay rates, that people are leaving for this reason and that matching rates paid by competitors would reduce turnover rates. Ideally, this would be supported by a strong business case showing that that current costs absorbed as a result of staff turnover are greater than those associated with the proposed pay rise (see Chapter 4).

The implementation issues associated with targeting pay rises at particular groups should not be underestimated. It is important not to create dissatisfaction amongst groups who are already fairly paid. The decision should be explained as openly as possible and any pay increase should be phased in at an appropriate time.

### Jephson Housing Association Group

In order to address a turnover rate of nearly 30% amongst administrators, Jephson introduced a salary acceleration scheme for this post. Under the scheme, staff have a 5% increase (subject to performance) each year to take them to a specified minimum salary in year three. This is a contractual entitlement and in addition to cost of living increases. Jephson report the initiative has been successful in contributing to an overall reduction in staff turnover, to well below 20%.

### Genesis Housing Group

Following major difficulties in recruiting and retaining professionally qualified, experienced Property Surveyors, a market review was undertaken. This determined a need to increase salary levels paid for qualified surveyors by £2,000. A non-contractual market supplement was introduced for all existing surveyors and for recruitment purposes.

Market supplements have been used within Genesis over several years to recognise fluctuations in the labour market for specific staff, and have resulted in successful recruitment and retention. This approach has tended to be used where there are immediate staff shortages, where waiting for the results of longer-term initiatives, such as in-house training programmes, is simply not an option.

## ❑ 12.4 Flexible benefits and total reward schemes

Even where it is unrealistic to pay the market rate, it remains possible for employers to attract and retain staff of the right calibre by improving the overall benefits package. This approach involves thinking about reward in the wider sense. It recognises that people value many things about their work, and may trade in a certain amount of potential pay in order to secure the other things that they value.

## ■ Flexible benefits schemes

Flexible benefits schemes, also known as 'cafeteria benefits' or 'flex plans', are formalised systems that allow employees to vary their pay and benefits package in order to satisfy their personal requirements.

They are not the same as voluntary benefits schemes (where employers arrange bulk discounts with external providers eg for vehicle breakdown cover) or net pay schemes (where employees pay for extra benefits).

There are several types of flexible benefits schemes:

- Total flexibility schemes – where employees can trade all benefits offered to them
- Core/peripheral schemes – core package plus flex account
- Mini flex/one off – limited number of options

The most usual scheme is a core package that everyone receives (eg basic pay, plus some pension, plus some holiday) but beyond this flexibility is permitted (eg staff can trade pay for more holiday) within the constraint of their total remuneration.

The aim for employers is to develop a package that competitors will find hard to replicate. The key requirements are:

- To design a pay and benefits package that is distinct from those offered by other employers
- To ensure that the benefits offered are genuinely appreciated by employees
- To minimise the cost of the package.

It is possible to design a simple scheme without the need for substantial investment. Following consultation with staff, it should be possible to design a number of 'set menus', including for example:

- For school leavers/graduates eg with emphasis on training
- For people with young children eg with an emphasis on childcare
- For people in their late 40s/50s, with emphasis on pension
- The existing standard package

### *Advantages of flexible benefits schemes*

- A competitive, flexible package will be valuable in attracting and retaining staff
- Employees are informed about the value of their benefits and the perceived value of benefits can increase

- Employees choose benefits to meet their needs and therefore value those benefits more highly
- Employers are seen to be more responsive to the needs of the workforce
- Dual career couples can avoid having benefits duplicated by their respective employers
- The awarding of benefits can become less divisive, especially where schemes are applied equally to all
- They have the capacity to defuse potential harmonisation problems when organisations merge or staff transfer across on different terms and conditions

### Potential disadvantages or difficulties associated with flexible benefits schemes

- Administrative complexity which carries an associated cost (although user-friendly IT systems are now available to help with costing and administration of such schemes)
- Good integration is needed between HR and payroll systems
- They are potentially confusing to employees

There is a considerable amount of guidance available on designing flexible benefits schemes (see Appendix 2).

### Considerations prior to implementing a flexible benefits scheme

- Consider fully the reasons for adopting this approach – if only limited flexibility is possible, it might be better to save the time and expense of introducing a full scheme and instead offer a more limited approach.
- Plan in advance – typically it will take 12 months to design and implement a scheme.
- Consider piloting a scheme, ensuring it is based on a representative sample of staff.
- Evaluate what the current package is worth and the level of understanding of it. Any new scheme must be considered within this context and should assess motivational as well as financial value.
- What will be the effect on the bottom-line pay bill?
- Survey staff as to the type of benefits they favour and value. However, care should be taken not to raise expectations that cannot be met.
- Offer benefits that give both the employee and their family a link to the organisation, broadening the emotional tie between employee and company.
- Ensure that benefits given on a 'family' basis eg pensions or private health insurance do not discriminate against same-sex couples.

- There must be a compromise between excessive flexibility that may encourage inappropriate choices and too narrow a choice that does not meet employee expectations.
- Is the internal culture ready? What will the union reaction be?
- Who will manage the scheme? What are the resourcing implications?
- Communication and education are key. If employees are aware of the reasons for and advantages of introducing flexible benefits they are less likely to dismiss it as a cost reducing exercise. Likewise it is essential that employees understand fully the benefits offered to enable them to make informed choices.
- In general, new schemes more likely to succeed if they are, in broad financial terms, cost neutral (ie with no overall gain to either employer or employee).

### Audit Commission

Each November, staff are given the opportunity to change their basic benefits package for the year ahead. Staff are entitled to:
- Buy or sell up to five days annual leave
- Buy various discounted insurance policies for self and family (including life insurance, critical illness cover, annual travel cover, pet insurance, permanent health insurance)
- Buy childcare vouchers
- Buy health plans and health screens.

### ■ Total reward perspective

Total reward may be regarded as the next logical step after flexible benefits have been implemented. Under a total reward policy, all aspects of the work experience are recognised and prominence is given not only to pay and benefits but also to less tangible rewards.

Items that might be included in a total reward scheme include:
- Pay and benefits (generally in the form of a flexible benefits scheme)
- Access to training
- Freedom and autonomy at work
- Opportunity for personal growth
- Recognition of achievements
- Preferred office space and IT equipment
- Flexible working hours

Advocates of total reward point to the importance that employees place on intangible rewards when deciding where to work and the level of commitment to give to their work. They stress the benefits of easier recruitment, reduced turnover, better business performance and an enhanced reputation of the organisation as an employer of choice

The perceived problems include:

- Complexity. There is no off-the-shelf package available to assist organisations.
- Clearly some rewards are more easily provided than others, and some are more quantifiable than others.
- It is argued that some 'rewards' are not an appropriate area for employee choice and should remain a purely business decision eg office accommodation or choosing a PC.

## ❏ 12.5 Recognition

One of the keys to improving morale and keeping the loyalty of employees is to ensure that staff feel valued. Recognition schemes (also known as non-cash rewards) are a visible way of rewarding achievement and of confirming that the contribution of an individual or team is important.

Recognition/motivational schemes might include:

- Thank you cards
- Personal call/visit/letter from Chief Executive
- Employee of the month award
- Staff awards ceremony
- Qualification achievement awards
- Attendance awards
- Celebration/outings/days off
- Retail vouchers

Points to consider:

- It is important to ask employees what they would value.
- Schemes should operate entirely separately from the pay and benefits package.
- Presentation and delivery of the reward can be as important as the reward itself (eg consider making the presentation at the staff conference and publicise details in the staff newsletter or intranet).
- Watch for tax implications. If the Inland Revenue classes a reward as an incentive, it is a 'benefit in kind' and therefore taxable.

........................................................................

## Bury Metropolitan Council

Bury Council launched its Employee Achievement Awards following a 'weak' assessment in its 2002 Comprehensive Performance Assessment. The council felt that the 'weak' tag did not reflect the good work that was going on across the council and the scheme was seen as one means of maintaining morale and celebrating successes.

The scheme aims to identify, recognise and thank those staff who 'go the extra mile' and there is a particular emphasis on people who have made a difference to the community. There are four team and four individual awards (one for each directorate) and an overall Employee of the Year Award.

Anybody who lives, works, visits or studies in Bury can get involved and council workers are able to nominate their colleagues. For example, employees in education have nominated social services staff for their support to people with learning disabilities.

An annual awards ceremony is held. Everyone who is shortlisted receives a certificate signed by the Mayor and Chief Executive and winners receive a shield and small prize.

........................................................................
........................................................................

## Irwell Valley Housing Association (IVHA)

IVHA, with the aim of inspiring and motivating colleagues, provides a range of benefits and rewards:
- Tailored, individual, personal and professional pursuit of excellence programme
- Lunch-time activities (eg yoga, singing lessons)
- Birthday cake and birthday off for good attendance over the year
- Incentives to stop smoking
- Support for gym membership
- Discounted contributions for dental and health care
- Free flu jabs, eye tests and cash help towards the cost of glasses
- Interest free loans
- Colleague days out
- Childcare vouchers
- Day off on child's first day at school
- Day off for grandparents on birth of first grandchild.

→

IVHA consider the positive benefits include:
- Improved performance
- Improved team working
- Reduced departmentalism
- Reduced stress, sick leave and turnover
- Increased colleague satisfaction – when surveyed 91% reported the benefits and working conditions were excellent
- Improved customer service – 93% satisfaction rate.

# CHAPTER 13

## WORKING CONDITIONS AND ENVIRONMENT

Dissatisfaction with working conditions and the working environment is a significant source of employee turnover. This chapter looks at initiatives organisations can adopt to improve the working conditions for their staff. It considers:

- Work-life balance/flexible working arrangements
- Equality in the workplace and tackling discrimination
- Dignity at work (addressing bullying and harassment)
- Reducing work-related stress
- Improving physical working conditions

## ❏ 13.1 Work-life balance/flexible working arrangements

The Work Foundation defines work-life balance as being about *"people having a measure of control over when, where and how they work. It is achieved when an individual's right to a fulfilled life inside and outside paid work is accepted and respected as the norm, to the mutual benefit of the individual, business and society."*

Over the past decade, the incidence of flexible working practices has increased substantially. These changes have been driven by the interaction of a number of important trends and events:

- The need for organisations to remain ahead in an increasingly competitive environment.

- Demographic changes and changes in the composition of the labour force, meaning that many more employees have caring responsibilities (for older people, as well as children).

- Introduction of legislation designed to tackle specific issues (eg the rights for parents to request flexible working arrangements under the Employment

Act 2002 and the protection against religious discrimination under the Employment Equality (Religion or Belief) Regulations 2003).

- A cultural shift in people's values and priorities, leading to increased demands for a better balance between work and personal life.

- The power and affordability of new technology (enabling homeworking).

The benefits of work-life balance are well documented and it is often described as a win-win situation. Research by the Industrial Society (now the Work Foundation) in 1998, found that 78% of employers believed that flexible working helped employees meet their domestic commitments more easily, and 80% that it also made the business run more effectively.

However, the protests that met the Employment Act 2002 revealed how much work-life balance is misunderstood. Work-life balance is about finding new ways for the organisation and for staff to work, which will make the organisation a better and more productive place. It is not just about increased rights for working parents. The right balance is important to everyone, whatever their age, situation or priorities outside work. As well as caring responsibilities, work-life strategies can assist with issues such as religious observance, health matters, disability, transport and travel to work, participation in arts, sports and education, participation in the voluntary sector and life planning (eg pre-retirement).

Improving work-life balance has the potential to be one of the most cost-effective methods by which employers can improve recruitment and retention. A survey of over 4,000 job seekers, carried out by Reed.co.uk on behalf of the DTI (2003) showed that a third of them would prefer the opportunity to work flexible hours rather than receive £1,000 more pay per year.

It is important to recognise also that informal gestures can be as effective as formal schemes. For this reason, work-life balance schemes are ideally suited to small businesses as well as larger organisations.

## ■ Flexible working – advantages

- Improved flexibility in the delivery of service to customers (eg more flexible hours for staff may be combined with longer opening hours or an evening surgery for tenants).

- Encourages creativity and innovation in the design and delivery of services.

- Improved recruitment through becoming an employer of choice, in comparison to competitors. The need to attract a younger generation to housing has been discussed, and there is evidence this group puts a higher premium on work-life balance.

- Flexible working can open up opportunities previously denied to certain sections of the community, eg disabled people or people with caring responsibilities.

- An effective work-life strategy is one of the ways in which equality for women and men at work can be promoted. Caring and other domestic responsibilities are among the key barriers to economic activity for women.

- Improved motivation and retention. Simple solutions can measurably improve loyalty, and unless a new employer can match a candidate's existing work-life balance provisions, they can be hard to give up.

- Potential for increasing performance.

- Reduced stress levels. Flexible arrangements can also help avoid a long-hours culture, which can ultimately lead to burn-out and resignations.

- Reduced sick leave and absenteeism, which are sometimes the last resort for people who have to care for dependents.

- Homeworking schemes can: reduce travelling time and costs; encourage cross-service working through location sharing; relieve the pressure on crowded office accommodation and reduce accommodation costs where 'hot-desking' is possible.

## ■ Flexible working – possible difficulties

- Some arrangements will not be possible for some staff (eg where tasks are time-critical or customer-facing) and this can seem unfair.

- The Sunday Times *100 Best Companies Survey* (2003) found a creeping feeling of discrimination amongst people without young children. This highlights the importance of making flexible working open to all employees where possible, not just those covered by legislation.

- There is the danger that a two-tiered workforce could be created unless schemes are properly monitored (see page 148 below). Valued employees with specialist skills may feel confident about approaching their managers and building a business case for changing their working patterns, but other individuals may feel less able to do so.

- In practice, take-up of schemes can be low. Kodz et al (2002) identified that concerns about career prospects caused much of the 'take-up gap'. Research for the JRF published by The Policy Press (2002) found a lack of awareness amongst staff of flexible arrangements in place in their company.

- If not properly planned, flexible working can sometimes lead to unexpected resourcing problems.

## ■ Range of flexible working initiatives
*Flexible hours schemes*

• • • • • • • • • • • • • • • • • • • • • • • • • • • • • • • • • • • • • • • • • • • • • • • • • • • •

### Royal Borough of Windsor and Maidenhead

The Borough's flexible working scheme includes a wide range of flexible hours arrangements:

- Flexitime
- Part-time working
- Job sharing
- Compressed working week/fortnight
- Annualised hours
- Term-time only contracts

in addition to homeworking and other family-friendly initiatives.

The scheme has been introduced with the purposes of meeting the increased demand from the public for greater flexibility in the provision of services, improving recruitment and retention and providing employees with a better work-life balance.

• • • • • • • • • • • • • • • • • • • • • • • • • • • • • • • • • • • • • • • • • • • • • • • • • • • •
• • • • • • • • • • • • • • • • • • • • • • • • • • • • • • • • • • • • • • • • • • • • • • • • • • • •

### United Welsh Housing Association (UWHA)

United Welsh is keen to promote work/life balance and has introduced a range of family-friendly initiatives, including term-time contracts allowing parents to care for children during school holidays.

• • • • • • • • • • • • • • • • • • • • • • • • • • • • • • • • • • • • • • • • • • • • • • • • • • • •
• • • • • • • • • • • • • • • • • • • • • • • • • • • • • • • • • • • • • • • • • • • • • • • • • • • •

### Northern Ireland Housing Executive (NIHE)

Following a successful pilot exercise, term-time working was introduced in the NIHE in 2003. Under this arrangement, part-time and full-time employees are allowed to take unpaid leave during the school holidays, or for another period, whilst retaining their permanent contract. Conditions of service, annual leave and salary are adjusted pro rata to the number of weeks worked. Salary continues to be paid in equal instalments over the normal pay period.

• • • • • • • • • • • • • • • • • • • • • • • • • • • • • • • • • • • • • • • • • • • • • • • • • • • •

### Family-friendly arrangements
Many flexible hours arrangements may of course be beneficial to employees with family responsibilities. In addition, employers may provide a number of schemes,

beyond statutory entitlement, aimed specifically at helping staff balance family and work commitments. Examples include:

- Dependency leave
- Parental leave
- Employer assisted childcare
- Support service (eg information on childcare or elder care options)
- Arrangements for grandparents

## SOHA Housing

SOHA sponsors TRIO, a local childcare network which provides staff with access to after-school and holiday clubs as well as registered child minders and nurseries.

### Flexi-place/teleworking/homeworking

Each of these terms is used to describe the process of people working away from the traditional office. Teleworking is generally used in situations where people are only able to carry out their duties with the use of technology such as networked computers and mobile telephones.

The Sunday Times *100 Best Companies to Work For Survey* (2003) found: *"The effect of homeworking was startling. If people are given just a bit of time to do their jobs from home – as little as one morning a week – their overall job satisfaction takes a gymnastic leap. Home workers rate employers higher in every area".*

## Aylesbury Vale District Council

AVDC introduced a Flexi-place scheme in 2000, which allows staff to work in the office, from home, on a mobile basis (on site), from other council offices or a combination of these.

The scheme was introduced with the following aims:

- To create more convenient working practices for staff, without any adverse effect on the service, customer care or productivity
- To aid recruitment and retention, by demonstrating a flexible attitude to staff
- To reduce commuting and congestion in Aylesbury.

# ■ Ensuring success of flexible working arrangements

- The culture of the organisation must create an environment in which work-life balance is recognised and valued and where individual responsibility and trust are encouraged. Performance and reward systems must be based on outputs, not hours present in the office.

- Flexible working schemes must be central to the organisation's aims and objectives. A key principle is that schemes should only encourage solutions which benefit the business as well as the staff. It should be approached holistically, with a view across all areas of the business, including HR, finance, IT and operations.

- A written policy is needed which is transparent and fair. Schemes must recognise the different needs of different people, and to this end, should avoid being over-prescriptive. Policies will work best if they increase flexibility rather than police it.

- Schemes must accommodate employees covered by employment legislation as a minimum but organisations should consider widening out schemes to include all employees.

- Schemes should not impose arbitrary restrictions. For example, a cut-off point by grade beyond which jobs cannot be worked flexibly could result in a glass ceiling preventing women from reaching senior positions.

- All arrangements must be checked for discrimination against particular groups of staff (eg do family-friendly working arrangements discriminate against same-sex couples?).

- The scheme should be developed in consultation with staff, customers and other relevant stakeholders. In particular, the involvement of line managers in policy design should help minimise any concerns over loss of control of resources.

- Employers should encourage creativity in ways of working and delivering the service and be open to suggestions from employees.

- Use of trial periods may confirm the practicality of particular arrangements and should prevent outright rejection of proposals.

- The scheme should be communicated widely, including at recruitment and induction stages. Good practice solutions and experiences should be shared internally. Staff should have access to advice on options.

- Line managers should be accountable for successful implementation. They will need to be equipped, (in terms of knowledge, understanding, resources and flexibility of approach) to be able to support work-life balance solutions. Work-life balance choices should not affect anyone's access to career development opportunities.

- Flexibility considerations should be built into reviews of posts eg when vacancies arise or when restructuring.

- All staff should be able to appeal against a decision (eg through grievance procedures) if they do not feel it has been given meaningful consideration.

- Where a request is refused managers should keep on file a record of the date, reason and circumstances of the refusal so that it can be reviewed at a later date. Employees should be given a timescale after which a new request will be considered.

- The success of work-life balance arrangements should be evaluated against the original business drivers (eg reducing staff turnover). This should include identifying and seeking to minimise any obstacles. Evaluation should include the effect of practices on staff, customers and performance.

- Take-up of work-life balance arrangements must be monitored. Over time, employers will gain a better insight eg into take-up by gender, ethnic origin, age or disability, position within the organisation and type of flexibility on offer.

- A commitment to continuous improvement is essential as both the needs of the business and the needs of individual staff members will change over time.

- Specific policies will be required for mobile/homeworking schemes, regarding use of technology, risk assessment, health and safety, confidentiality and tax and other liabilities.

A large body of guidance and best practice is available from government and other agencies (see Appendix 2).

···········································································

## Bromford Housing Group

Bromford was voted the Best Employer for Work and Family in the 2003 *Sunday Times 100* list.

The principles behind the Group's flexible working framework are trust, flexibility and the need to measure outputs. The framework, which is just two pages long, does not contain detailed prescription. Managers are given a 'green light' to agree flexible arrangements with their staff, provided:

- People work their contracted number of hours
- There is no compromise on essential service delivery
- There is no compromise on performance
- Colleague relationships are not adversely affected, both within and between teams
- Arrangements are agreed in advance and not at the last minute.

···········································································

························································································

## Telford and Wrekin Borough Council

The council's working arrangements have led to them receiving the BT Carers in Employment Award and the NSPCC-sponsored family-friendly award.

The Borough has one of the highest concentrations of single mothers in Europe and, as roughly 80% of the workforce is female, they support a range of initiatives that enable mothers to return to work. These include:

- Assistance with childcare costs
- Workplace crèche
- Local shop discounts
- Nursery hotline for those needing emergency childcare
- Flexible working hours.

Flexible arrangements are open to all staff and 52% now work part-time. Line managers handle individual requests and are encouraged 'to use common sense and be caring in a practical way'. They are expected to initiate work-life balance conversations and act as role models by looking after their own work-life balance.

Since introducing flexible practices, the council has been able to operate for an extra three days each year and for longer hours. They report that sickness levels and turnover have dropped and that staff loyalty and morale have improved.

························································································

## ❏ 13.2 Equality in the workplace and tackling discrimination

Employers have a moral duty to eliminate discrimination in the workplace. In addition, there are significant implications for business performance, as a result of demoralisation, stress and anxiety experienced by victims, possibly leading ultimately to resignation. Further, the costs of legal action, tribunal proceedings and compensation can be considerable. Damage to reputation is an additional factor.

The Employment Equality Regulations 2003, which ban discrimination in the workplace on the grounds of sexual orientation and religious belief, have brought the issues of workplace discrimination and equality to the fore for many organisations. Similar protection against discrimination on the grounds of disability and age is forthcoming (see Appendix 1).

The 2003 Regulations work in a similar way to the long-standing laws on sex discrimination and race relations. They should assist employers to look more broadly at how they acknowledge and celebrate diversity in the workplace and to deal with the prejudices that exist within organisations. At the same time, there is much organisations need to do to ensure they are complying with the existing and forthcoming legislation.

The practical issues for employers include:

- The need to review all HR policies and working practices to ensure they are not treating staff less favourably on the grounds of race, sex, age, disability, religious or other belief or sexual orientation.
- In particular, in respect of religious discrimination laws, managers need clear policies on issues such as holidays, religious observance and dress code.
- Training is important. HR departments and line managers should understand the issues that particular groups of staff are likely to face (eg older workers, followers of particular religions or lesbian, gay or bisexual people). All employees should receive general awareness training in these areas.
- It is important to create a culture where staff feel confident to raise issues and they should be encouraged to do so. There is an anomaly for lesbians and gay men who are not 'out' at work, making it difficult for them to claim an entitlement or bring a complaint. The best way forward is to create a climate where lesbians and gay men feel that it is safe to come out.
- Consider staff/management network groups focusing on areas such as race, disability or faith. These will help individuals to raise issues and will also let the organisation know whether policies are working.
- Under the 2003 Regulations, there is no requirement to keep monitoring information on religion or sexual orientation. However, if organisations decide to include this in their monitoring processes, staff must be told why such information is being collected, how it will be used and that giving such information is voluntary. All such information should be confidential and anonymous and is designated 'sensitive' under data protection legislation.

Note: The issue of workplace harassment is addressed below in the dignity at work section.

........................................................................................

## ASRA Greater London HA

ASRA Greater London HA, a mainstream association with BME specialism, has been addressing the cultural issues of religious diversity within their organisation for many years. They aim to balance cultural and religious needs with operational demands to deliver effective services. Practices include:

- Granting time off for prayers and special consideration given if staff are fasting
- Flexitime system allowing employees to join their families in fast-breaking
- Allowing staff to participate fully in religious activities during working hours eg provision of a quiet room for prayers, for people of all faiths
- Allowing staff to take annual leave during religious festivals or to take longer periods to celebrate religious events abroad

→

- Providing a 'personal day' as leave, which can be used at any time of the year for religious or other purposes
- Avoiding work events on key religious dates
- Permitting traditional dress at work
- Special arrangements concerning the food, and food storage, provided at work
- Alcoholic drinks prohibited except with the consent of those affected.

## Positive Action in Housing (PAIH)

In response to the Employment Equality Regulations 2003, PAIH have developed a religious leave policy whereby up to three days religious leave may be awarded to address faiths not covered under public holidays. The policy clarifies that religious leave is distinct from annual leave and that if religious leave is not taken on the day of the festival it cannot be transferred to another day. Similarly, if the festival takes place at the weekend or a public holiday, then leave cannot be transferred to another day.

Both ACAS and the BBC provide useful information on particular religious traditions. A training pack assisting employers to deal with discrimination on the grounds of sexual orientation is available from Lesbian and Gay Employment Rights (LAGER).

## ❏ 13.3 Dignity at work

The term 'dignity at work' is increasingly used in connection with harassment and bullying. Research published in IRS Employment Review (2002) revealed that bullying and harassment were the most common causes of complaint at work, overtaking pay and conditions.

Research in 2003 by Barony Consulting suggests that the housing sector lags behind many other professions when it comes to tackling harassment at work. Levels of non-reporting were high and 13% of staff had no confidence that their employer would take effective action against bullying or harassment.

People may be harassed or bullied because of their sex, race, disability, religion, beliefs, nationality, age, sexual orientation, physical characteristics or personal circumstances. Following the Employment Equality Regulations 2003 (see above), a key area that employers need to address is that of offensive banter in the workplace eg religious jokes or homophobic comments. Employers will be liable for acts of their employees, unless they can prove they have taken steps to prevent the employee's acts.

---

### Good practice checklist: Tackling harassment and bullying

Organisations need to ensure:

✓ They promote awareness amongst staff of what is, and what is not, acceptable behaviour and the impact unacceptable behaviour can have on colleagues.

✓ They have in place clearly defined and communicated policies on the organisation's stance towards harassment and bullying.

✓ They are able to quantify the extent and nature of bullying and harassment in the organisation, in order that they can begin to address it. Organisations may consider using a harassment index, a measure of the level of harassment by source and type, gathered from anonymous staff questionnaires. The index can be used for harassment health checks, designing interventions and measuring effectiveness of interventions.

✓ Staff are equipped with the skills to challenge unacceptable behaviour.

✓ They promote a climate in which employees feel valued and sufficiently supported to bring forward complaints without fear of recrimination.

✓ Clearly defined reporting mechanisms are in place and there are procedures for dealing with matters promptly and sensitively, taking into account the rights of both parties.

✓ The victim has access to confidential counselling, advice and support.

✓ Training is in place for those involved in applying the policy.

✓ They monitor the effectiveness of the policy and training, involving staff in any such review.

---

From a retention perspective, what is important is the perception of staff. Written policies, procedures and assurances about the organisation's stand on these matters are insufficient, if staff see things differently. Organisations have to ensure they are quite clearly seen to be addressing these issues.

## Horizon Housing Group

Horizon HG provides compulsory Dignity at Work training for all staff. The training addresses the concepts of bullying and harassment, the legal background, the Group's own dignity at work policy and organisational good practice, and engages staff in group work and case studies.

The organisation reports that the training has resulted in a more open environment where colleagues are more ready to come forward with complaints of harassment or bullying and are more confident that their complaints will be taken seriously.

A *Ban Bullying at Work Action Pack* has been produced by the Work Foundation, addressing the needs of employers, individuals and trade unions.

# ❏ 13.4 Stress

The Health and Safety Executive (HSE) defines stress as *"the adverse reaction people have to excessive pressure, or other types of demands, placed upon them. It arises when they worry that they cannot cope"*.

MORI research in 2003 amongst employees of housing associations found 34% of staff reporting that stress within the workplace affected their personal life and almost as many saying it affected their job performance (30%). Middle managers reported most stress at work. The research also found a strong link between stress and dissatisfaction with the job.

There is a compelling case for organisations to deal with stress in the workplace:

- Organisations have a moral obligation to not make their staff ill by putting them under excessive pressure.
- Employers are obliged, under health and safety legislation, to recognise and manage occupational stress.
- The cost, in terms of staff absence and turnover, can be huge. Research by the Employers' Organisation for Local Government shows that stress accounts for almost 20% of all reported ill-health absence and over 33% of all long-term absences.
- Organisations also run the risk of legal costs, large compensation pay-outs and damaged reputation if they are sued for damages or if formal action is taken by the HSE. Depending on the circumstances, they may also expose themselves to claims such as constructive dismissal, unfair dismissal or a discrimination claim. A passive approach to workplace stress by the employer is likely to be fatal to the defence in any such action/claim.

---

### Good practice checklist: Employers' responsibility to tackle stress

✓ Have in place a written risk assessment of all health and safety hazards in the workplace, including occupational stress. This is a legal requirement. It should be updated annually.

✓ Consider an auditing approach to measuring stress levels. HSE draft guidance on tackling workplace stress advises employers to collect the views of their staff in a quantitative way, followed by more detailed qualitative assessments (eg through focus groups) to discuss with staff the specifics of their stressors.

✓ Have in place a Stress Policy, detailing how the identified risks are to be managed and reduced or eliminated. Some organisations choose to promote a more proactive Well-Being Policy, recognising the need to maximise the well-being of their employees rather than merely reduce their stress.

✓ Train managers in identifying and managing stress and how to work with employees to address stress.

→

---

✓ Develop a supportive work ethos, with senior commitment, to encourage staff to discuss and seek support when experiencing stress.

✓ Offer counselling or support. Many organisations provide a confidential counselling and legal advice telephone service for employees.

✓ Consider offering stress management and relaxation techniques training.

✓ Promote healthy behaviour and exercise. Consider giving staff access within work time to stress-relieving therapies such as massage or acupressure.

### Sadeh Lok Housing Group

Sadeh Lok, a BME association with 38 staff, employs a life coach. The visits are parts of a Staff Care programme that includes talking over problems, setting goals, managing time better and building confidence. Sadeh Lok has successfully passed the Health and Safety Stress Standard.

The Health and Safety Executive is producing management standards intended to help employers understand what is expected of them in managing work-related stress, and to allow them to monitor and improve their own performance in this area. Other sources of guidance for employers on managing organisational stress are given in Appendix 2.

## ❏ 13.5 Physical working environment

Job dissatisfaction is likely to result where the physical environment is unsuitable or uncomfortable to work in (eg due to overcrowding, noise, poor temperature control, inadequate lighting, lack of privacy or lack of security).

The working environment is particularly crucial for staff, such as those working in call centres, habitually using equipment such as VDUs and headsets. There is increasing recognition of the need for ergonomically designed furniture, frequent breaks and interaction with other staff.

There is a need to consider how facilities and services (eg rest rooms or catering facilities) reflect the cultural diversity of the workforce.

Health and safety hazards should be addressed via the risk assessment procedure outlined above. It is good practice to consult employees regularly about their environment and to involve them in decisions about office refurbishment or redesign of their own workspaces.

# CHAPTER 14

## FUTURE DIRECTIONS

These are significant times for the housing sector. Over the next decade, changing demography, rising customer expectations, and the demands of government initiatives, will bring further change to the sector. At the same time, organisations need to be responding to a new era in people management. As well as new flexible working laws, major changes are taking place in discrimination law, with new and expanding protection for employees. The aspirations of employees, and their awareness of their statutory rights, are increasing steadily.

It is clear that some of the more traditional ways of working are unsustainable and that new approaches are required. Many of the barriers to new approaches are embedded in a culture of working practices that have gone unquestioned for many years. Recurring themes are the need in the sector for a culture of greater inclusivity, flexibility and willingness to accommodate.

In such a fast-changing environment, housing organisations need dynamic and effective leadership. The various sector-wide initiatives under way (see Chapter 2) illustrate that the sector is waking up to a chronic lack of investment in this area in the past. Individual organisations too need to examine their approach to leadership development and succession.

The Housing Corporation's Leadership 2010 initiative refers to the need to 'break the mould' when it comes to recruiting and developing future housing leaders. It stresses the need for a more diverse leadership, capable of working in different and more flexible ways. It sees an opportunity as many of the older leaders in the sector start to retire in the next decade, and has set stringent targets with regard to the appointment of women and people from BME backgrounds.

The strong business case for improving diversity at all levels throughout the sector is well documented. The Government is also leading in this area, through an integrated, comprehensive approach to equality issues. There are plans to replace the three specialist equality bodies – the Equal Opportunities Commission, the Commission for Racial Equality and the Disability Rights Commission with a single umbrella organisation – the Commission for Equality and Human Rights. The government's new vision for equality is clearly 'protection for all', not separate agendas for different minority groups. As well as ensuring equality legislation is easier to use to provide redress for individuals, the new Commission will have an active role in promoting equality in employment and service delivery.

It is crucial for organisations to recognise that it is not enough to improve diversity in recruitment. Recruiting from a more diverse pool of people will have implications for, amongst other things, induction and training, career development, work-life balance and working environment. For diversity initiatives to be sustainable, many organisations will need to concentrate their attentions in these areas.

Also high on the Government's agenda is work-life balance. Following the Employment Act 2002, the Government was expecting 500,000 parents to make requests for flexible working by April 2004. They have made it clear that if there is widespread evidence that the legislation is being ignored, they will consider some test of objective justification or even some guarantee of the right to flexible working.

The demographic trends that in part underlie the increase in flexible working are set to continue. People Management magazine reported in July 2003 that: *"In the next 10 years, the workforce will grow by 1.5 million, of which 85% will be women. 78% of women with school age children work outside the home. Some 22% of workers expect to have care responsibilities for older people within the next 5 years"*.

Over the next ten years the number of flexible workers is forecast to grow by 400%, at which point 25% of the workforce will be working flexibly.

As people's aspirations increase, in terms of their expectations of working life, organisations are likely to find they need to go beyond the statutory framework to make flexible working effective.

An important element of the NHF's 'iN Business' initiative is the encouragement of collaborative working. Partnership ventures in the sector in the areas of recruitment, training and development do not seem to have been widely explored, and could provide real opportunity for organisations. All too often employers in the sector are fiercely competing for talented staff, to the extent that employees are blamed for leaving and rival organisations are accused of poaching staff. Research shows that the majority of current staff want to stay with their employer and, that those who do want to move wish to remain within the sector. Organisations need to be looking at what they can do collectively, as well as individually, to attract staff and enable them to stay.

One thing is certain, whether working individually or in partnership with others. It will be essential to invest in a commitment to continuous improvement, as both the needs of the organisation and the needs of individual employees will continue to change over time.

# Appendix 1

## Summary of Relevant Current and Forthcoming Legislation

### ❏ Equality

#### The Sex Discrimination Act (SDA) 1975

The SDA makes it unlawful to discriminate against an employee, directly or indirectly, on the grounds of sex or marital status. The legislation does allow for the use of positive action in a number of specified circumstances, to counter the effects of past discrimination or disadvantage.

Under EC regulations, amendments to UK sex discrimination laws must be implemented by 2005. Amongst other things, sexual harassment will be treated as unlawful sex discrimination.

#### The Equal Pay Act 1970

The Act makes it unlawful to discriminate between men and women in their contracts of employment including pay, holiday entitlement and pension. The Equal Pay regulations were extended in April 2004, to give employees considering pursuing a claim, the right to obtain relevant information from their employer so enabling them to decide whether to implement proceedings.

#### The Race Relations Act (RRA) 1976

The RRA makes it unlawful to discriminate, directly or indirectly, on grounds of colour, race, nationality, ethnic or national origin. The legislation does allow for positive action in specified circumstances, to counter the effects of past discrimination or disadvantage.

#### The Race Relations Act 1976 (Amendment) Act 2000

The 2000 Act prohibits racial discrimination in all public functions, with only a few limited exceptions. It also places a statutory duty on listed public bodies to promote race equality. In addition, the listed public bodies are bound by the employment duty to monitor by ethnic group their existing staff and applicants for jobs, promotion and training and publish the results every year. Those bodies with at least 150 full-time staff must also monitor grievances, disciplinary action, performance appraisals, training and dismissals. (Local authorities are listed public bodies in the Act, but housing associations are not).

## The Race Relations Act 1976 (Amendment) Regulations 2003

The Race Regulations 2003 introduced, amongst other things, a new, broader definition of indirect race discrimination and a new, statutory definition of racial harassment.

## The Disability Discrimination Act (DDA) 1995

The DDA makes it unlawful for an employer to treat a disabled person less favourably than a non-disabled person, for a reason relating to their disability, in respect of: selection, recruitment, promotion, training, terms and conditions of employment, other benefits (such as pensions), dismissal, or by subjecting the employee to other detriments (such as harassment).

It is not automatically illegal for an employer to discriminate against a disabled person. However, the employer must justify the discrimination and must have considered making 'reasonable adjustments' to their work tasks, workplace, working arrangements or recruitment processes to ensure the disabled employee or applicant is not placed at a 'substantial disadvantage'.

The Disability Discrimination Act 1995 (Amendment) Regulations 2003, effective from 1 October 2004, will make significant changes to the DDA. The main changes are:

- The removal of the exemption from the DDA for small (fewer than 15 staff) employers
- Changes to the meaning of discrimination and harassment.

A Draft Disability Discrimination Bill was published in December 2003. The Bill will extend the DDA to cover almost all areas of the public sector, including local authorities. It will strengthen existing DDA rights in the areas of: definition of disability, transport services, renting premises and discriminatory job advertisements. It will also introduce a new duty on public bodies to promote equality of opportunity for disabled people (similar to the race equality duty).

## Employment Equality (Religion or Belief) Regulations 2003

The Regulations prohibit direct and indirect religious discrimination and harassment and victimisation. Religion is defined as being any religion, religious belief or similar philosophical belief. The Race Relations Act 1976 protects employees against religious discrimination only to the extent they can establish they belong to an ethnic group. A main impact of the 2003 Regulations is to provide clear protection against discrimination for the Muslim community. Compensation for religious discrimination claims is unlimited. Employers are liable for the acts of their employees.

## Employment Equality (Sexual Orientation) Regulations 2003

The Regulations prohibit both direct and indirect forms of discrimination and harassment and victimisation on the grounds of sexual orientation. The two main areas in which sexual orientation discrimination legislation is likely to impact are workplace harassment of gay people and benefit packages that exclude same-sex couples or discriminate in favour of married employees. Compensation for sexual orientation claims is unlimited. Employers are liable for the acts of their employees.

## Age Discrimination

In the context of employment, the most significant aspect of the EC Anti-Discrimination Directive (No.2000/78), to be introduced in the UK by 2006, is its prohibition of discrimination on grounds of age. There is currently no legislation of this kind in Britain. The key implications are likely to be the prohibition of arbitrary age ranges for recruitment and the end of compulsory retirement ages.

# ❑ Family-friendly legislation

## The Employment Relations Act 1999

The Act gives working parents the right to unpaid parental leave and time off to deal with emergencies.

## The Employment Act 2002

The Act contains a range of measures to enhance maternity and parental rights. In addition, it gives parents of children under 6 (under 18 in the case of a disabled child) the right to apply for flexible working arrangements and to have their employer seriously consider that request.

Subsequent legislation is likely to refine elements of the core flexible working legislation, focusing particularly on paternity needs and also further defining reasonable parameters for work-life balance.

# ❑ Data protection

## Data Protection Act 1998

The Act provides comprehensive protection for individuals in relation to the use or processing of personal data about them.

The Information Commissioner has produced an Employment Practices Data Protection Code, a wide-ranging code of practice on the use of personal data in employment relationships.

The EC is proposing to overhaul the regulation of data protection.

# ❏ Working time

## The Working Time Regulations 1998

These Regulations set a limit on how many hours people can work.

There are likely to be significant changes to working-time laws in the UK in future years. The UK is under threat of legal action by the EC that it has failed to properly transpose the requirements of the EC Working Time Directive into UK Law. In addition, the EC has indicated that it wants the provision in the UK Regulations, which allows individuals to 'opt out' of the 48-hour week, deleted from the Directive.

# ❏ A-typical working arrangements

## The Part-Time Working Regulations 2000

These Regulations require employers to offer the same terms and conditions pro rata to part-time workers as full-time workers.

## Fixed-Term Employees Regulations 2002

The Regulations prevent discrimination against fixed-term employees in their terms and conditions (including pay and pensions).

# ❏ Record checking

## Asylum and Immigration Act 1996

Since January 1997, it has been a criminal offence to employ someone who is not entitled to work in the UK. An employer can apply for a work permit to employ a person who is not entitled to work in the UK. The Government has introduced changes from 1 May 2004, to the types of document which employers need to check to avoid employing illegal workers.

From 1 May 2004, nationals from countries in the expanded European Union are allowed to work in the UK. Nationals from eight of these new EU countries are required to register with the Home Office.

## The Rehabilitation of Offenders Act (ROA) 1974

Under the ROA, it is unlawful to take into account 'spent convictions' in recruitment, promotion and dismissal situations. Some categories of job are exempt from the ROA, the effect being that an individual must disclose spent convictions if asked about their criminal record. These categories include working with vulnerable adults and working with children.

# Human Rights Act (HRA) 2000

The HRA protects the human and civil rights of individuals and has a potential impact on working practices and policies.

## ❏ Miscellaneous

### Union and employee representation

Following the EC National Works Council Directive, employees in the UK will have new rights to information and consultation. These must be implemented by March 2005.

### Transfers of Undertakings (Protection of Employment) Regulations 1981 (TUPE)

Reforms, including clarification on when TUPE applies, are expected to come into force on 1 October 2004.

### Employment status

A major review of employment status in relation to statutory employment rights is under way. This may result in an extension to the scope of statutory employment protection for people such as agency workers and casual workers.

The Government proposes to provide agency workers with greater protection from exploitation and enable them to move more easily from temporary work to permanent employment. Further direction from the EC on agency workers is expected.

### Dispute resolution

From 1 October 2004, the Government is introducing new legislation to encourage settlement of employment disputes within the workplace with a view to reducing pressure on the employment tribunal system.

Note: there are a number of statutory provisions affecting only local government which local authorities need to be aware of when recruiting staff. A summary of these is provided by the Employers' Organisation www.lg-employers.gov.uk

**Appendix adapted from *Employment Law Update for Social Landlords*, Lewis Silkin Solicitors, 2003**

# APPENDIX 2

# REFERENCES AND SOURCES OF FURTHER INFORMATION

## ❑ Chapter 1

### References

Sunday Times (2003) *100 Best Companies to Work For Survey*

The Sunday Times (2004) *100 Best Companies to Work For Survey*

The Sunday Times (2004) *50 Best Small and Medium-Sized Enterprises (SMEs) To Work For Survey*

The Financial Times (2004) *50 Best Workplaces in the UK*

## ❑ Chapter 2

### References

Labour Market Statistics (April 2004)

CIPD (2003) *Recruitment and Retention Survey*

ONS (September 2003) *Economic Trends* No.598

Institute for Employment Research (April 2001) Brief No. RBX08-01

Equality Direct website www.equalitydirect.org.uk

Housing Corporation, RSR 2003 data

Housing Corporation (2003) *Leadership 2010: The Way Forward*

Audit Commission (2002) *Recruitment and Retention – a public service workforce for the twenty-first century*

Housing Potential (2000) *Labour Market Information and Skills Foresight Report*

Genesis Housing Group (2002) *To Have and To Hold: Staff Recruitment and Retention in Housing Associations* (summarises MORI research)

MORI (2003) *Staff Retention in Housing Associations* to be summarised as a Housing Corporation *Sector Study* autumn 2004, will be available online www.housingcorplibrary.org.uk

Roffey Park Institute (2001) *Roffey Park Management Agenda*

Purcell, John (2003) *People and Performance: unlocking the black box*, CIPD

Taylor, Stephen (2002) *The Employee Retention Handbook*, CIPD

ODPM (2004) *Egan Skills Review*

Barker, Kate (March 2004) *Review of Housing Supply – Delivering Stability: Securing our Future Housing Needs.* Available from the Treasury website – www.hm-treasury.gov.uk

Housing Today (19 Sep 2003)

ODPM News Release (25 September 2003) *PFI and transfer strengthens Government Decent Homes target*

Inside Housing (12 December 2003)

## Sources of further information

iN Business for Neighbourhoods www.inbiz.org

Housing Corporation (2003) *Leadership 2010: The Way Forward* www.housingcorplibrary.org.uk

CIH Leadership Programme for Housing www.cih.org/training/leaderdev.htm

Bright Futures, Bright Lives, Bright Careers: www.brightfutures.uk.com

Inside Housing and Trotman *Getting into Housing* Contact: 0870 900 2665

Housing Corporation Recruitment Forum: contact for further information is 020 7393 2000

NHF Recruitment, Retention and Retraining Group: contact for further information is 020 7067 1010

Chartered Institute of Housing/The Housing Corporation (2001) *Neighbourhood Management: A Good Practice Guide*

Asset Skills: the Sector Skills Council for the property services, housing, cleaning and facilities management sectors. Email enquiries@assetskills.org

## ❏ Chapter 3

### References

Institute for Employment Studies (2002) *A New Way of Looking at Leadership*

Taylor, Stephen (2002) *The Employee Retention Handbook*, CIPD

Purcell, John (2003) *People and Performance: unlocking the black box*, CIPD

MORI (2003) *Staff Retention in Housing Associations* to be summarised as a Housing Corporation *Sector Study* autumn 2004, will be available online www.housingcorplibrary.org.uk

## Sources of further information

Age Positive is the Government's campaign to tackle age discrimination and promote the business benefits of age diversity in the workplace: www.agepositive.gov.uk

Eden Brown offers a free booklet on the implications of age diversity legislation for organisations. Download at www.edenbrown.com or to order hard copy email agepositive@edenbrown.com

Dialog, the diversity team at The Employers Organisation for Local Government www.lg-employers.gov.uk/diversity provides a wide range of information on diversity issues

Lesbian and Gay Employment Rights (LAGER) www.lager.dircon.co.uk

Equality Direct www.equalitydirect.org.uk

The Equal Opportunities Commission (EOC) website includes guidance on legislation for employers, codes of practice, positive action and equalities monitoring www.eoc.org.uk

The Commission for Racial Equality (CRE) website includes information on the duty to promote race equality, equal opportunities policies, ethnic monitoring, code of practice for employment and contains advice specific to the housing sector www.cre.gov.uk

The Disability Rights Commission (DRC) website includes information for employers on legislation, recruitment, induction and training, career development, monitoring disability, and includes information for small organisations www.drc-gb.org

There are various tools available to help organisations audit their current performance:

- Housing Race Equality Toolkit (De Montfort University) www.dmuracetoolkit.com
- Employers' Organisation *Equality Standard for Local Government* www.lg-employers.gov.uk/diversity
- *Race Equality: A Framework for Review and Action* (NHF) www.housing.org.uk

*Equality in Housing: A Code of Practice* (NHF) supplemented by a series of guidance providing advice on tackling discrimination in a variety of fields including race, gender, disability and sexual orientation www.housing.org.uk

*Leadership Development: What works?* www.lg-employers.gov.uk

Investors in People (IiP) *Leadership & Management Model* www.investorsinpeople.co.uk

ACAS (April 2003) *Employee Communications and Consultation* www.ecacas.co.uk

The Employers' Organisation for local government produces guidance on developing employee communication strategies www.lg-employers.gov.uk

*The Experience of Black and Minority Ethnic Staff* (2002) Chartered Institute of Housing in Scotland www.cih.org/home_scotland

Communities Scotland (2003) *Precis* No 27 *Good practice in Positive Action*

# ❏ Chapter 4

## References

Audit Commission (2002) *Recruitment and Retention – a public service workforce for the twenty-first century*

Employers' Organisation for local government website: Improvement and Capacity Development section www.lg-employers.gov.uk

CIPD (2003) *Labour Turnover Survey*

Taylor, Stephen (2002) *The Employee Retention Handbook*, CIPD

Genesis Housing Group (2002) *To Have and To Hold: Staff Recruitment and Retention in Housing Associations* (summarises MORI research)

MORI (2003) *Staff Retention in Housing Associations* to be summarised as a Housing Corporation *Sector Study* autumn 2004, will be available online www.housingcorplibrary.org.uk

## Sources of further information

CIPD *Employee Attitude and Opinion Surveys* www.cipd.co.uk

The Employers' Organisation for local government provides guidance on developing attitude surveys and leavers' questionnaires, including sample questions www.lg-employers.gov.uk

# ❏ Chapter 5

## References

Genesis Housing Group (2002) *To Have and To Hold: Staff Recruitment and Retention in Housing Associations* (summarises MORI research)

MORI (2003) *Staff Retention in Housing Associations* to be summarised as a Housing Corporation *Sector Study* autumn 2004, will be available online www.housingcorplibrary.org.uk

## Sources of further information

Forum 3 Recruitment and Volunteering Event: www.forum3.co.uk

The Education Business Partnerships (www.nebpn.org) and The Trident Trust (www.thetridenttrust.org.uk) work to create links between schools, business and the wider community.

The Careers Research Advisory Council (CRAC) and Industrial Society Education (www.crac.org.uk/indsoc/14_19/school_conferences.htm) run a programme of School Conferences, which aim to promote interaction between the future workforce and those currently employed in a wide variety of industries.

Reading Borough Council *New Deal for Housing Project* Tel: 0118 939 0900

Warden Housing Association *Good Practice Guide on Local Labour in Construction* Tel: 020 8868 9000

Housing and Employment Working Group (2002) Final Report and Recommendations *Maximising employment opportunities through housing* www.communitiesscotland.gov.uk/web/FILES/MaximisingEmployment.pdf

Communities Scotland (2002) *Precis* No.16 *Measuring the impact of RSL Employment Initiatives: Using the Wider Role Framework*

Organisations that can assist with volunteering include:
 – CSV (Community Service Volunteers): www.csv.org.uk
 – National Centre for Volunteering: www.volunteering.org.uk
 – the local Council for Voluntary Service which coordinates voluntary activities in each area.

For Equality/Diversity references see Chapter 3.


# ❏ Chapter 6

## References

Investors in People UK (2002) *Recruitment and Selection Model*

CIPD (1998) *Recruitment: Key Facts*


## Sources of further information

CIPD (2003) *Quick Fact: Competency and Competency Frameworks* www.cipd.co.uk

The Employers' Organisation for local government produces guidance on producing competency frameworks www.lg-employers.gov.uk


# ❏ Chapter 7

## References

Cubiks (2001) *Predicting the workplace of 2010*

Workthing (2003) *E-recruitment study*


## Sources of further information

Hays Montrose and Association for Public Service Excellence (APSE) have produced a step-by-step guide to using and developing temporary recruitment services within local authorities: *Temporary Recruitment – Best Practice: Solutions and Strategies*

Further information on the service available from Jobcentre Plus is available at www.jobcentreplus.gov.uk

People Media Ltd, online recruitment specialists in the not-for-profit sector, provide guidance on: *Writing copy for the web* and *How to promote your Careers*. www.peoplemedia.co.uk

Graduate Opportunities for Local Government (GOLD) www.lg-employers.gov.uk

# ❏ Chapter 8

## Sources of further information

Guidance on conducting interviews is available from ACAS www.acas.org.uk

Further information on testing is available from:
- British Psychological Society (BPS) www.bps.org.uk
- CIPD *Quick Fact: Psychological Testing* (June 2001) www.cipd.co.uk
- Saville and Holdsworth provide internet recruitment and assessment systems including psychometric testing www.shl.com
- Property People Publications (2003) *Psychometric Testing for the Housing Sector* www.ppmagazine.co.uk

The Employers' Organisation for local government guidance on medical checks is available from www.lg-employers.gov.uk

Home Office Guidance on the prevention of illegal working is available from www.ind.homeoffice.gov.uk

Information on criminal records checks is available from the Criminal Records Bureau www.crb.gov.uk and www.disclosure.gov.uk

# ❏ Chapter 9

## Sources of further information

PATH National Ltd www.pathuk.co.uk

For more information on Modern Apprenticeships, contact the Learning and Skills Council www.lsc.gov.uk

For more information on Construction Training Opportunities, contact the Construction Industry Training Board (CITB) www.citb.co.uk

Gee+ scheme: contact East Thames Housing Group 020 8522 2000

HERA New Entrants Scheme www.hera-group.co.uk

National Graduate Development Programme (NGDP) www.lg-employers.gov.uk

Association of Graduate Recruiters (AGR) www.agr.org.uk

# ❏ Chapter 10

## References

CIPD (2003) *Recruitment and Retention Survey*

Industrial Society (1997) Managing Best Practice 38: *Induction*

CIPD (2003) *Quick Fact: Induction*

## Sources of further information

ACAS produces guidance on induction, including an induction checklist www.acas.org.uk

CIPD produces several reports/publications on induction, including an example checklist www.cipd.co.uk

The Diversity Team at the Employers' Organisation produces guidance on diversity issues in rural areas www.lg-employers.gov.uk/diversity/race

Disability Employment Advisers (DEAs) at the Dept for Work and Pensions (DWP), provide advice on any aspect of employing disabled people. They can be contacted via local Job Centre Plus.

The Career Opportunities for Ethnic Minorities (COFEM) mentoring training and process package is available from the Housing Corporation website www.housingcorp.gov.uk

The National Mentoring Network (NMN) promotes the development of mentoring, offers advice to those wishing to set up mentoring programmes and provides a forum for the exchange of information and good practice www.nmn.org.uk

The Housing Projects Training Service Tel. 01942 682620

# ❏ Chapter 11

## References

Purcell, John (2003) *People and Performance: unlocking the black box*, CIPD

Genesis Housing Group (2002) *To Have and To Hold: Staff Recruitment and Retention in Housing Associations* (summarises MORI research)

MORI (2003) *Staff Retention in Housing Associations* to be summarised as a Housing Corporation *Sector Study* autumn 2004, will be available online www.housingcorplibrary.org.uk

## Sources of further information

The CIPD's Library and Information Services has copies of secondment policies from a range of different organisations, both public and private www.cipd.co.uk

A number of organisations provide support with secondment to the voluntary sector, including:
- Business in the Community www.bitc.org.uk
- Employees in the Community Network www.volunteering.org.uk/workwith/eitcn.htm

Information on the range of qualifications and training for the housing sector is available from the Chartered Institute of Housing:
- Housing qualifications  education@cih.org
- Distance learning courses  dlc@cih.org
- Training and conferences (includes in-house training service) training.conferences@cih.org

Further information on COFEM and details of regional COFEM groups are available via the Housing Corporation website www.housingcorp.gov.uk

Federation of Black Housing Organisations (FBHO) www.fbho.co.uk

Learn Direct produces a Director's Briefing on Personal Development Plans www.learndirect.co.uk

# ❏ Chapter 12

## References

Employers' Organisation for local government website: Pay and Reward section

## Sources of further information

ACAS produces guidance on Appraisal Related Pay, Job Evaluation and Pay Systems: www.acas.org.uk

Further information is available from the Pay and Rewards Section of the Employers' Organisation for local government website www.lg-employers.gov.uk

CIPD (2002) *Quick Fact: Flexible Benefit Schemes* www.cipd.co.uk

The Work Foundation (2000) Managing Best Practice 75 *Flexible Benefits* www.theworkfoundation.com

# ❏ Chapter 13

## References

Industrial Society (1998) Managing Best Practice 46 *Flexible work patterns*

Reed.co.uk on behalf of the DTI (2003)

Sunday Times (2003) *100 Best Companies to Work For Survey*

The Policy Press in association with JRF (2002) *Employed carers and family-friendly employment policies*, summarised in JRF Findings 972

Personnel Today (10 September 2002) *Bullies fight way to top employee complaints* (IRS research)

Barony Consulting (2003) *Making Work Life Balance Work*

Employers' Organisation press release (4 Sep 2003)

IES (2002) *Work-life balance: beyond the rhetoric*

HSE Website www.hse.gov.uk/stress

## Sources of further information

Barony Consulting Group/Housing Corporation *Making Worklife Balance Work* Toolkit, produced by www.wlbforhousing.org.uk

The Work-Life Balance website, provided by The Work Foundation, provides help, information, a benchmarking tool and case studies www.employersforwork-lifebalance.org.uk

The Work Foundation (2003) Managing Best Practice 109 *Work-life Balance* www.theworkfoundation.com

The Work Foundation (May 2003) *Time to go Home: Embracing the Homeworking Revolution* www.theworkfoundation.com

Investors in People UK: Work-Life Balance Model – offers guidance on setting up effective work-life balance policies www.investorsinpeople.co.uk

TUC provides practical advice on achieving a better balance in the workplace www.tuc.org.uk/changing times

Guidance from DTI: www.dti.gov.uk/work-lifebalance and www.dti.gov.uk/er/workingparents.htm

The Employers' Organisation for local government produces model policies on work-life balance issues www.lg-employers.gov.uk

Chartered Institute of Housing/The Housing Corporation (1999) *Teleworking: A Good Practice Guide*

ACAS *Guide to the Employment Equality (Religion or Belief) Regulations 2003* provides information on particular religious traditions www.acas.org.uk

Housing Today (28 November 2003) *Tolerance isn't enough* article on religious diversity in the workplace

The BBC offers useful information via its Religion and Ethics pages www.bbc.co.uk/religion

A training pack assisting employers to deal with discrimination on the grounds of sexual orientation is available from Lesbian and Gay Employment Rights (LAGER).

ACAS has produced a Guide to the Employment Equality (Sexual Orientation) Regulations 2003 www.acas.org.uk

Stonewall Employer's Champion Network is a forum in which employers can work with Stonewall to promote diversity in the workplace www.stonewall.org.uk

The Work Foundation (2002) *Ban Bullying at Work* Action Pack www.theworkfoundation.com

Bully Online website provides information, support and links www.bullyonline.org

www.raceactionnet.co.uk is an online resource providing good practice on tackling racial harassment

HSE Management Standards for Work-Related Stress (in draft form as at May 2004) www.hse.gov.uk/stress

HSE (2003) *Real Solutions, Real People – a Manager's Guide to tackling Work-related Stress.* This Guide is based around case study interventions that have been effective in other organisations www.hsebooks.co.uk

Robertson Cooper *Beacons of Excellence in Stress Prevention* available from www.hsebooks.co.uk

Employers in Voluntary Housing *Understanding Stress* a booklet which includes sample risk assessment forms and an example stress policy www.evh.org.uk

CIPD (February 2003) *Quick Fact: Stress* www.cipd.co.uk

# ❏ Chapter 14

## References
People Management (10 July 2003) *How to effect changes to working hours*